D1145950

BIG PANTS,
BURPY AND
BUMFACE

BIG PANTS, BURPY and BUMFACE

RUSSELL ASH

DOUBLEDAY

BIG PANTS, BURPY AND BUMFACE
A DOUBLEDAY BOOK 978 0 385 61723 9

Published in Great Britain by Doubleday,
an imprint of Random House Children's Books
A Random House Group Company

This edition published 2009

1 3 5 7 9 10 8 6 4 2

Mixed Sources
Product group from well-managed
forests and other controlled sources
www.fsc.org Cert no. TT-COC-2139
© 1996 Forest Stewardship Council

RANDOM HOUSE CHILDREN'S BOOKS
61–63 Uxbridge Road, London W5 5SA

www.**kids**at**randomhouse**.co.uk
www.**rbooks**.co.uk

Addresses for companies within The Random House Group Limited can be found at:
www.randomhouse.co.uk/offices.htm

THE RANDOM HOUSE GROUP Limited Reg. No. 954009

A CIP catalogue record for this book is available from the British Library.

Printed and bound in Great Britain by Clays Ltd, St Ives plc

*Whether you thank them or blame them,
this book is dedicated to anyone whose
parents gave them an unusual name.*

Contents

· · · · · · · · · · · ·

Introduction

1. Weird and Wonderful Names 20

2. Incredible Insults 38

3. Strange Science 49

4. Curious Creatures and Puzzling Plants 72

5. Marvellous Monsters and Myths 95

6. Bizarre Bodies, Dotty Diseases and Dead Ends 99

7. Toilet Titters 116

8. Freaky Food and Daft Drinks 123

9. Home Humour 143

10. Comical Clothing 151

11. More Weird and Wonderful Names 157

12. School Silliness 176

13. Potty Playtime 179

14. Mind-boggling Music and Silly Sounds 184

15 Batty Battles and Crackpot Criminals 191

16. Mad Moves 198

17. Preposterous Places 205

18. Perfect Pairs 216

19. Peculiar Puritans 226

20. Name Games 232

21. The Name's the Same . . . 256

22. Even More Weird and Wonderful Names 279

23. Crazy Calendar 301

24. Astonishing Afterthoughts 312

25. Amazing Americans 315

Introduction

What's this book about?

This book is all about strange names. Anyone could sit down and make up a lot of funny names, but what's special about these is that they are all real! Every one of the people here once had to answer the everyday question 'What's your name?' with something like, 'Perfect Perfect', 'Preserved Fish' or 'Pleasant Bottom'.

It is reckoned that the six billionth baby on Earth was born on 12 October 1999, and the seven billionth will be born in 2012. In the past 50,000 years of human life, there have been perhaps as many as 100 billion people on the planet, and since language began, every one of them has had a name – even if it was as simple as 'Ug'.

First names, also called given names because they are the names our parents give us, have been around since ancient times – Matthew, Mark, Luke and John and many other names we all know appear in the Bible. Surnames, or family names, are those with which we are born. They are more recent, dating back only about 1,000 years – although not every culture has them. One thing they do is to help us tell one person from another – imagine how hard it would be if every boy was called John Smith and every girl Mary Smith, although in England there have probably been more people with these pairs of names than any others.

So parents often come up with something different, and sometimes with something that is so different or so strange that it makes us laugh – I'll bet you have never met anyone with names like Hippo, Grasshopper or Cabbagestalk, or full names such as Oofty Goofty Bowman, Goolsby Scroggins, Grouchy Gangloff, Pincus Elephant or Minnie Fart. But they all exist or have existed.

How did they get these names?

In choosing a name for their newborn baby, parents have often created a problem by going for a first name or initial that doesn't go well with the surname, for example Stan Still, Rhoda Boat, Chris P. Bacon or T. Hee. Many of them mean something else, perhaps because a child's parents had not thought carefully enough about what it would sound like, so we get names like Annie How, Ina Hurry, Easy Pease, Henrietta Postman, Lew Swires, Agusta Wind, Lorna Mower, Hans Up, and girls with the first name 'Ima', such as Ima Lady, Ima Man, Ima Nutt and Ima Pigg. Or they have come about because language has changed, so that a name that was once quite ordinary now means something different to us – like Lou Paper, Ham Burger, Barb B. Doll and Wendy House. Some of these might not be totally obvious at first. Try saying them out loud!

Then there are cases where a woman marries and so changes her name, sometimes ending up with something very odd. When Wild Rose married a Mr Bull she became Wild Bull; Love Bowden married Charles Beer and became Love Beer; and recently, when Truly Gold married Cary Boring she became Truly Boring!

Sometimes it works the other way round: though not always true today, it was once usual for women to always take their husband's name when they married, so their children would have a different surname and their own would be 'lost'. Also, people who were unfortunate enough to have embarrassing surnames like Bottom or Smelly often changed them legally to something less rude.

What are not included are the sometimes strange names that famous people give their children, such as chef Jamie Oliver's daughters Poppy Honey, Daisy Boo and Petal Blossom Rainbow, or singer Gwen Stefani's son Zuma Nesta Rock, or names that people have because they changed their original names to something crazy, like Toasted T. Cake or Jellyfish McSaveloy. These were deliberate, to attract attention or make someone stand out in a crowd (sometimes for a bet, and often regretted afterwards), but most of the names in the book were accidental.

Of course, no one is suggesting that any of these names were or are bad names – some, such as Sunny Day, are rather lovely, or wonderful – as in the case of Wonderful Ramsbottom; but many of them are surprising, unexpected and funny.

How to use this book

Each name is accompanied by evidence to show that it was real. That might come from a record of birth, marriage or death, a census (an official record of everyone who lived in a place on a particular day) or some other source. In this information, there are some commonly used abbreviations:

c. – circa *(Latin for about)*, *means that only the approximate year is known*

Jr – *this means Junior, the son of someone with the same name*

Sr – *stands for Senior, the elder of two people with the same name*

née – *French for 'born', the name a woman had before she changed it by marriage*

[sic] – *Latin for 'so', meaning that even though the spelling looks wrong, it is correct*

Taking the three names that give us the title of the book, this is the sort of information we discover about them:

Big Pants
(Male) Born c.1863 (Pine Ridge,
Dakota Territory, 1886 US Indian census)

Censuses – official counting of all inhabitants –
take place in most countries every ten years. In
Britain we can study records from censuses from
1841–1911 and in the USA from 1790–1930.
In the USA from 1885 to 1940 there were also
separate censuses of Native American tribal people,
then called 'Indian censuses'. Big Pants was a
member of the Sioux tribe. It says 'Male' as it's not
obvious from his name whether he was male or
female – although we don't always know. He was
living in Dakota Territory in the USA at the time
of the 1886 Indian census (the states of North and
South Dakota did not exist until 1889). His exact

14

birth year is not known, but he was said to be 23, so we can calculate it was about 1863. From the census return (the form filled out to show who was living and where), we also discover that Big Pants had a younger sister called Red Woman and a brother called Pretty Eagle. For other names from America, remember that the country was a collection of colonies and then states until 1776, when it became the United States of America, or USA, so 'America', not 'USA', is used for events before that year.

Ricard Burpy
Born 5 May 1816; baptized Wesleyan Methodist, Frome, Somerset, 26 October 1817

Here we know both the exact birth date and the

name of the church where Ricard (an old spelling of 'Richard') was baptized or christened. Church records go back hundreds of years – some of the earliest names in the book come from them. Baptisms were usually carried out when a baby was a few days old (Ricard was unusual in being more than a year old), so even if the birth date was not recorded, it helps us know the approximate year of birth. This took place in England – unless it says otherwise (such as 'Scotland' or 'USA'), all the names in the book are from England or the United Kingdom.

Albert Bumface
Married Léontine Victorine Florence Silvestre, Paris, 29 October 1871

Some of the names in the book come from countries other than England and the USA, like this marriage record from France. By marrying Albert, poor Léontine became known as Madame Bumface.

Other sources

Other sources of information include lists of passengers and crew on ocean liners travelling from one country to another – perhaps immigrants to the United States. Their names, ages and the place where they came from were often listed. Another source is draft registrations: soldiers' names and birth details were recorded when they were drafted, or recruited into the army. The place where they were drafted is listed, which may or may not be the same as the place they were born. Some names come from wills – before a person dies, they often make out a will, an official document in which they say what should happen to their possessions after their death. Some of the names come from these documents, and even if we do not know much more about the person, they were carefully checked by lawyers and can be relied on as accurate.

Not all these records are accurate: mishearing a name, illiteracy and uncertainty about spelling (even a name as famous as William Shakespeare has been spelled in twenty or more different ways!) and human error in writing them down means that a few names may be mistakes!

Where did I find all these names?

Not so long ago, if you wanted to write a book like this, it would have been much more difficult. To find names in birth, marriage and death registers or censuses, you would have to go to the actual records in a special library and look them up in thousands of big, heavy volumes. To do the same in the USA, you would have to go to each of the fifty states and do the same. If you worked very hard, you might find enough names to make a book – but it would take many years. Then the Internet happened.

One of the most popular uses of the Internet is family history, or genealogy (you can find out about it in books such as Emma Jolly's *Family History for Kids*, 2007). Gradually, birth, marriage, death and census records for many countries – especially the UK and USA – have been made available online, so now it is a relatively simple task to look up names and get the details. As a result, people all over the world have been able to trace their ancestors and discover their family trees.

Most of the websites charge for access, but there are some very good ones that are free, so why don't you start off by trying:

FreeBMD
(www.freebmd.org.uk)
and
International Genealogical Index
(www.familysearch.org)

Who knows, you may find a seventeenth-century person with your name – and if you find a funny one, do please tell me!

Russell Ash
Lewes 2009
www.RussellAsh.com

Weird and Wonderful Names

● ● ● ● ● ● ● ● ● ● ● ● ● ● ● ● ● ● ●

Emperor Adrian

Born St James', Clerkenwell Green, London, 7 May 1809

'Emperor' was his first name.

B. Ann Angel

(Female) Born Bedwelty, Monmouthshire, 1894

Eileen Back

Born Merthyr Tydfil, Glamorgan, 1908

Ed Banger

Baptized North Petherton, Somerset, 4 February 1635

Dewey Barefoot

Born 19 July 1903; died Banks, Alabama, USA, July 1984

*He was one of six people with the same name whose deaths
were recorded in the USA between 1970 and 2000.*

Faith Hope And Charity Barratt

Born Exeter, Devon, 1846

'Faith Hope And Charity' were her first names.

John Goto Bed

Born London c.1822 (Swanage, Dorset, 1861 England census)

Felix Bigarre Bizarre

Born Essex, Ontario, Canada, 3 August 1870

Fairy Blessing
Born 20 November 1899; died York,
Pennsylvania, USA, April 1970

Fleno Bobo
Born 15 February 1912; died Mississippi,
USA, 29 August 1990

Wincenty Bonk
Born 23 July 1892; died Wilmington, Delaware,
USA, March 1971

Qumeller Boone
Born 3 January 1925; died Indiana, USA, 22 March 1989

Ima Box
Born Missouri c.1904 (Washburn, Missouri, 1920 US census)

Ina Box
Born Tennessee c.1897 (Humphreys, Texas, 1910 US census)

Ivory Box
Born 7 August 1908; died East St Louis, Illinois,
USA, November 1982

Tarzan Branch
Born 27 February 1922; died Alexandria,
Virginia, USA, 24 April 2008

Zelophehad Broadbear
Born Axbridge, Somerset, 1854

Ernest Winkle Bunn
Born Wolstanton, Staffordshire, 1892

Philadelphia Bunnyface
Laneast, Cornwall (recorded in a will, 1722)

Tim Burr
Born Watford, Hertfordshire, 1867

Sylvan Cabangbang
Born 7 February 1900; died Darien,
Connecticut, USA, March 1969

E. Normus Carpenter
Born 25 May 1866; died Boise,
Idaho, USA, 3 November 1936

Fred Caveman
Born Germany 1828 (Cincinnati, Ohio, 1900 US census)

Bobby Watt Cheek
Born Catawba, North Carolina, USA, 25 March 1937

Crystal Clear
Married William Travis, Pasquotank,
North Carolina, USA, 1969

Cletus Clodfelter
Born Troutman, North Carolina, USA, 25 October 1921;
died Troutman, 1 August 1958

Henry Whitney Clapsaddle
Born New York 1 January 1896
(Herkimer, New York, 1910 US census)

Bendy Corner
(Male) Born Stoke Damerel, Devon, 1892

C. Cret
Born c.1872 (Pratt, West Virginia, 1930 US census)

Robert H. Crucifix
Born City of London 1852 (Kensington, 1881 England census)
*His name is an example of 'nominative determinism', a name
that is right for a person's job, as Robert H. Crucifix was a
clergyman. He used the middle initial 'H' as he probably felt
his actual name, 'Harmer', sounded less appropriate.*

Salome Cruncher
Born Stratford, Nottinghamshire, c.1841
(Newington, London, 1881 England census)

Possible Dadson Dadson
Born Croydon, Surrey, 1991

Dansey Dansey
(Male) Baptized St Helen's, Worcester,
18 September 1800

Earwacker Deadman
Born Alton, Hampshire, 1849

Poppy Bizarre S. Devereux
Born Trowbridge, Wiltshire, 1995

Ding Ding
Died Thanet, Kent, 30 April 1971

All Done
Born Derby 1898

Ben Dover
Baptized St George in the East, London, 10 March 1839

Eileen Dover
Born 1924; died Swindon, Wiltshire, 1987

Ida Down
Born Okehampton, Devon, 1894

Neil Down
Born 19 December 1914; died Port Huron,
Michigan, USA, 13 April 1991

Trufly Dubey
Born Michigan *c*.1892 (Buckeye, Michigan, 1910 US census)

Hugh Dunnet
Born Scotland *c*.1836
(Dinsdale, Durham, 1861 England census)

Barb Dwyer
Born California *c*.1896 (Oakland, California, 1920 US census)

Gladys Rose Early
Born Wandsworth, London, 1899

Layton Early
Born Kentucky c.1827 (St Clair, Missouri, 1850 US census)

Sundance Starmoon S. Elgar
Born Lewisham, London, 1988

Sir Dusty Entwistle
Born Bury, Lancashire, c.1877 (Bury, 1881 England census)
'Sir Dusty' were his first and middle names.

Eva Faithfull
Born Winchester, Hampshire, 1895

Wave Feather
(Male) Born Windsor, Berkshire, c.1825
(Hampton, Middlesex, 1851 England census)

Haldeman Figyelmessy
Born Philadelphia, USA, 7 February 1880
(First World War draft registration)

Adam U. First
Born Pennsylvania 1866
(Conneaut, Pennsylvania, 1900 US census)

Rhoda Fishback
Born Louisiana c.1875 (Burke, Louisiana, 1920 US census)

Nancy White Flagg
Born Worcester, Massachusetts, USA, 7 January 1811

Regena Flooz
Born c.1919 (Chicago, Illinois, 1930 US census)

James Fluffy
Born Iowa c.1860 (Des Moines, Iowa, 1910 US census)

Larkin Fooshe
Born 8 December 1910; died Richmond,
Georgia, USA, 28 March 1995

Doctor Septimus Forrest
Born Preston, Lancashire, c.1834
(Blackburn, Lancashire, 1851 England census)
He was probably a seventh son – they were once
believed to have magical powers and,
especially in Lancashire, were often
given the first name 'Doctor'.

George Tweet Foster
Born Mattingley, Hampshire, c.1870
(Heckfield, Hampshire, 1891 England census)

William Danger Fripp
Born Bristol, Gloucestershire, c.1879
(Bristol, 1901 England census)
He could rightly say 'Danger is my middle name . . .'

Phifer Fullenwider
Born North Carolina c.1887
(Monroe Union, North Carolina, 1910 US census)

Serious Funny
Born South Carolina c.1872
(Georgetown, South Carolina, 1930 US census)

Truthful Futty
Born Stockton-on-Tees,
Durham, 1867

Opportune Ganwit
(Female) Born France c.1842
(Shirburn, Oxfordshire, 1871 England census)

Forget-me-not Geeves
Born Hertford 1898

Dan Ger
Born Devon c.1796
(Roborough, Devon, 1841 England census)

Glamour Girl
Married Robert H. Travers, Edmonton, London, 1960

Nice Go
(Female) Born China c.1923; passenger on
President Taft, Hong Kong, China–Madera,
California, USA, arrived 1 March 1938

Rhoda Goodsheep
Married Dudley, Staffordshire, 1874

Lung Googoo
(Male) Born c.1896; passenger on *Montrose*, Antwerp,
Belgium–Quebec, Canada, arrived 8 May 1913

Anna Gram
Born c.1811 (Ambrosden, Oxfordshire, 1841 England census)

Excess Green
Born 1 September 1899; died Houston, Georgia,
USA, 15 March 1970

Notwithstanding Griswold
(Female) Born Durham, Connecticut, USA, 16 April 1764

Peter Handsomebody
Baptized St Andrew's, Holborn, London, 19 February 1758

Hannah Harmless
Married James Eston, Byford, Herefordshire, 13 October 1829

Sweet Hart
Died St Mary Newington, London, 1837

Fluffy Heaver
Born 1901; died Kensington and Chelsea, London, 1998

T. Hee
(Male) Born Nafferton, Yorkshire, c.1891
(Great Driffield, Yorkshire, 1901 England census)

Doug Hole
Born Manchester, Lancashire, c.1910
(Manchester, 1911 England census)

Elizabeth Curious Horn
Born Oklahoma 1894; married Albert Herbert Whiteshield,
12 October 1912; died 19 December 1914
She was the daughter of Curious Horn and Little Woman.

Sufferana How
Born Watertown, Massachusetts, America, 1620;
died 22 July 1692

Alice Surprise Hutchinson
Born Islington, London, 1883

May Igo
Born Illinois c.1861 (Chicago, Illinois, 1880 US census)

Frothy Jackson
(Female) Born Markington, Yorkshire, c.1831
(Potternewton, Yorkshire, 1901 England census)

Thomas Jellyblood
Of Easton in Gordano, Somerset (recorded in a will, 1590)

Babegirl Nicole Ruth Jones
Born Cardiff, Glamorgan, 2006

Excellent Evidence Kambissi
Born Islington, London, February 2004

Joe King
Married Alice Adams, North Mimms,
Hertfordshire, 15 April 1668
*He must have got fed up with people saying
'You must be Joe King . . .'*

Win King
(Female) Born Lancashire c.1839
(Manchester, Lancashire, 1841 England census)

Bent Korner
Born c.1921; crew on *Guayana*, Vancouver, Canada–Everett,
Washington, USA, arrived 14 September 1949

Industrious Kubb
(Female) Born Chelsea, London, c.1806
(Wandsworth, London, 1881 England census)

E. Lastic
Born 16 September 1923; died Ohio, USA, July 1972

Ernest Laughter
Born Bromsgrove, Worcestershire, c.1880
(Bromsgrove, 1881 England census)

Lorraine Popoola Leak
Born Manchester, Lancashire, 1988

I. Level
Born Glasgow 10 December 1859

Lily Lightbrown
Baptized St Luke's, Preston, Lancashire, 21 December 1892

Ima Longnecker
Born Iowa 1893 (Collins, Iowa, 1900 US census)

True Love
Born Newington, London, 1848

A. Little Lowder
Born Kansas, USA, 31 July 1877
(First World War draft registration)

Epiphany Lullaby
Married Veryan, Cornwall, 3 January 1767

Major Major
Born Islington, London, 1871

Minor Major
Born Missouri c.1898 (Jackson, Missouri, 1910 US census)

Ima Man
Born c.1919 (Provo, Utah, 1930 US census)

Shane Rubber Man
Born 19 May 1944; died Hartford,
Connecticut, USA, 28 March 2001

Handy Mann
Died Croydon, Surrey, 1860

Knowledge Mann
(Male) Born Kenn, Devon, c.1863
(Newton Abbot, Devon, 1881 England census)

Ewan Mee

Born Nottingham 2000

Mercy Mee

(Female) Born Loughborough, Leicestershire, 1880

Minnie Mee

Born Derby 1873

Pebble Miracle

Born 19 November 1928; died Detroit, Michigan,
USA, December 1984

Harmless Montgomery

Born 29 January 1902; died Hoxie, Arkansas, USA, May 1975

Fice Mork

(Male) Born New York, USA, 29 April 1909; died New York
February 1969

Salome Mud

Born Mile End, London, c.1876
(Bethnal Green, London, 1891 England census)

Oscar L. Mumpower

Born Virginia c.1915 (Goodson, Virginia, 1920 US census)

Alice Neate-Price

Born Nottingham 1994

Arthur Nightmare

Born Shelby, Michigan, USA, 23 May 1881

Venus Officer

Born 1 November 1901; died Chicago,
Illinois, USA, 5 October 1994

Alpha Omega
(Male) Born Mexico 1 October 1940; died
Los Angeles, California, USA, 21 July 1987
*Alpha and Omega are the first and
last letters of the Greek alphabet.*

Gladys Over
Born Foleshill, Warwickshire, 1898

Emily Odd Paste
Married West Ham, Essex, 1882

Lula Peepless
Born Georgia c.1893 (Davenport, Iowa, 1930 US census)

Moral Person
Born 30 September 1923; died Palmyra,
New Jersey, USA, 19 October 1989

Per Person
Born 7 February 1900; died Manchester, Connecticut,
USA, January 1979

Tiny Person
(Female) Born North Carolina c.1909
(Hayesville, North Carolina, 1910 US census)

Vaseline Person
Married D. C. Love, Madison, Tennessee, USA, 3 April 1924

Mene Mene Tekel Upharsin Pond
Born Connecticut, America, 5 March 1721

Coco Pope
Born Cheltenham, Gloucestershire, 2005

Wee Girlie Potter
Born Risbridge, Suffolk, 1906

Mayoress Kate Preston
Born Brentford, Middlesex, 1880
'Mayoress' was her first name.

A. Quaintance
Born 29 October 1917; died Boulder, Montana,
USA, 20 February 1998

Pacifico Quitiquit
Born 25 January 1900; died Seattle,
Washington, USA, May 1968

Eva Ready
Born New York 1874 (Antwerp, New York, 1900 US census)

Hughe Relief
Born Stackpole Elidor, Pembrokeshire, c.1579

Sapphire Ring
Born Derby 1980

Tommy Rot
Born Shoreditch, London, 1871

Velveteen Sailors
Born 15 April 1927; died Tucker,
Georgia, USA, 19 January 2004

Shadrack Scarrott
Born Evesham, Worcestershire, 1891

Goolsby Scroggins
Born 27 January 1900; died St Louis,
Missouri, USA, December 1971

Sosthenes Sille
Born 4 August 1921; died Schenectady,
New York, USA, 16 March 2008

Boleslaw Slam
Born 6 May 1878; died Pennsylvania, USA, March 1964

Tiny Small
Born c.1918 (Cass, Missouri, 1930 US census)

President Percy Smith
Born Poplar, London, 1882

Wonderful Smith
Born Blything, Suffolk, 1893

Arabella Snoot
Married Shaftesbury, Dorset, 1838

Zenas Spaceman
Born Chesterton, Cambridgeshire, 1861

John Spong Spong
Born Maidstone, Kent, 1842

Moriah Hope Picaboo Sprinkel
Born Hennepin, Minnesota, USA, 11 February 2000

Purple Starkweather
(Male) Born Connecticut c.1781
(Milton, Vermont, 1850 US census)

Rollin Stone
Born 19 May 1896; died Ringgold,
Georgia, USA, 31 May 1987

Flossy May Strike
Born Aylsham, Norfolk, 1890

Fare-well Sykes
Born Honley, Yorkshire, 1842

Fare-well was one of the four sons of Sydney and Betty Sykes.
Fare-well, who drowned in 1865, was the brother of Live-well,
Do-well and Die-well Sykes.

Ann Teak
Ann, *née* Morley, married William Teak, Rothwell,
Yorkshire, 22 May 1722

Ida Threewits
Born 4 July 1890; died Bakersfield,
California, USA, April 1982

May Kal Tay Not A Ting
(Male) Born Minnesota c.1888
(Cass, Minnesota, 1910 US census)

The census record for May Kal Tay Not A Ting also includes
Sah Jah Ja Way Jat Low, Kay A Gat Nook A Bia Cis,
Thom Jah Not Ammy Ke and other strangely named children.

T. Towel
Married Deborah Handsley, Freiston,
Lincolnshire, 13 May 1783

Vera Horsey Trott
Born Weymouth, Dorset, 1901

Page Turner
Born Axminster, Devon, 1865

Fred Umbrella
Born Essex c.1875 (Danbury, Essex, 1881 England census)

Maximum Velocity
Married Teresa N. Hanks, Coventry, Warwickshire, 1999

Sallie Long Walkingstick
Born North Carolina, USA, 10 December 1864

Luke Warm
(Female) Born Ely, Cambridgeshire, c.1891
(Ely, 1901 England census)

Preservation West
(Male) Baptized Melksham, Wiltshire, 25 September 1627

Blacken White
(Male) Born Tennessee c.1892
(Lawrence, Tennessee, 1920 US census)

Valiant Wigington
(Male) Born Hull, Yorkshire, c.1861
(Sculcoates, Yorkshire, 1881 England census)

Andrew Willibother
Citizen of Patapsco, Maryland
(1790 US census)

Fairy Wingo
Born 5 March 1912; died Dallas, Texas, USA, 1 October 2001

Betsy Witch Witch
Baptized Ringwood, Hampshire, 1 September 1772

Chip Wood
Born Huddersfield, Yorkshire, 1867

Liza Wrong
Baptized St Margaret's, Westminster,
London, 11 February 1618

Oldest Young
(Male) Born Alabama c.1907
(Jefferson, Alabama, 1920 US census)

Incredible Insults

● ●

Elizabeth Barmy

Married William King, Letheringsett, Norfolk, 1702

John Bigass

Born Detroit, Michigan, USA, 5 May 1887

Hannibal Bighead

Born Oklahoma *c*.1888 (Lincoln, Oklahoma, 1910 US census)

Idiot Bigmeat

Born 1877 (North Carolina, 1918 US Indian census)

Joe Bignose

Born Minnesota *c*.1880 (St Louis, Minnesota, 1910 US census)

Vera Boring

Born Alabama *c*.1908 (Thompson, Alabama, 1910 US census)

John Brainless

Born Durham *c*.1863 (Durham, 1891 England census)

Nutty Bullock

Born North Carolina *c*.1858
(Townsville, North Carolina, 1880 US census)
Her grandmother was another Nutty Bullock.

Albert Bumface

Married Léontine Victorine Florence Silvestre,
Paris, France, 29 October 1871

Dick Bumshead
Born Lambeth, London, c.1828
(Westminster, London, 1891 England census)

Naughty Burkhammer
(Female) Born 1894; died Weston,
West Virginia, USA, 14 January 1939

Stinky Burhouse
Born Holland c.1823 (Spring Lake, Michigan, 1870 US census)

Obese Burke
Born Louisiana c.1902 (Lafourche, Louisiana, 1920 US census)

Calamity Burkes
(Male) Born Arkansas c.1900
(Union, Arkansas, 1910 US census)

Bernard Daft Butler
Born Prescot, Lancashire, 1907

Num Butt
Born Iowa c.1911 (Manhattan, New York, 1911 US census)

Lazy Card
(Female) Born Tunbridge Wells, Kent, c.1868
(Tunbridge Wells, 1871 England census)

Depression Carter
(Male) Born North Carolina c.1871
(Blues Sand Hill, North Carolina, 1910 US census)

Mean Chav
Born 5 September 1933; died Rochester,
Minnesota, USA, 10 November 2006

Eva Childish
Born Maryland c.1853 (Baltimore, Maryland, 1880 US census)

Misery Constant
Born North Carolina c.1898
(White Oak, North Carolina, 1910 US census)

Alice Crackers
Born Hull, Yorkshire, c.1871
(St Margaret, Leicestershire, 1891 England census)

Alderman Cranky
Married Lydia Woodby, Boston, Suffolk,
Massachusetts, USA, 28 December 1742

Imbecile Crazy
Born c.1846 (Utah, 1887 US Indian census)

Daffy Dingle
Born Delaware c.1835 (Baltimore, Delaware, 1880 US census)

Michel Disgust
Resident of New Orleans (Louisiana, 1860 US census)

Vile Ditto
(Male) Born 5 May 1910; died Lima,
Ohio, USA, 12 January 1960

Major Dork
(Male) Born North Carolina c.1845
(Cheraw, South Carolina, 1880 US census)

Polly Drunkard
Married Benjamin Lewis, Madison,
Kentucky, USA, 16 June 1796

Peculiar Dukes
(Female) Born c.1923 (Wynne, Arkansas, 1930 US census)

Edeltraud Robinson Dumfart
Born Austria c.1929; passenger on *Vulcania*, Genoa,
Italy–New York, USA, arrived 29 October 1949

Troublesome John English
Born England c.1897; passenger on *Demerara*, Buenos Aires,
Argentina–Liverpool, UK, arrived 23 October 1922

Hopeless Evans
Born Stoke-on-Trent, Staffordshire, 1880

Soo Fat
Born 1 August 1903; died Hong Kong February 1974

Magdalena Fatty
Born 8 June 1919; died Mescalero, New Mexico,
USA, 16 February 1997

Tom Fool
Baptized Chorley, Lancashire, 13 January 1706

George Gaga
Born c.1847 (St Pancras, London, 1871 England census)

Semi Gaga
(Male) Born Naruwai, Fiji, c.1896

Grouchy Gangloff
Born 20 August 1902; died Gonzales,
Louisiana, USA, January 1973

John Ghastly
Born Pennsylvania c.1909
(Gettysburg, Pennsylvania, 1930 US census)

Constant Grief
Born *c*.1907 (Paducah, Kentucky, 1930 US census)

Constance Grumble
Born York 1913

Ruenette Grumbly
Married George Morris, Tuscola,
Michigan, USA, 17 February 1876

Mad Hatter
Born Wigginton, Oxfordshire, *c*.1879
(Northfield, Worcestershire, 1901 England census)

Big Head
Born California *c*.1857 (Fresno, California, 1860 US census)

Edwin M. Headcase
Born Grasmere, Westmorland, *c*.1867
(Toxteth Park, Lancashire, 1891 census)

Sarah Horrible
Married Winchester, Hampshire, 1848

Angry Howard
Born 1 May 1892; died Louisiana, USA, August 1965

John Idiot
Married Hailsham, Sussex, 1848

Irving Imbecile
Born New York *c*.1913 (Bronx, New York, 1930 US census)

Crazy Jim
Born 18 July 1933; died Milwaukee, Wisconsin,
USA, 16 March 2002

Dirty King
Died Hatfield, Hertfordshire, 1863

Putrid Ida Kirk
Born Tennessee *c.*1835 (Maury, Tennessee, 1930 US census)

Messy Licker
(Female) Born Chorley, Lancashire, *c.*1803
(Manchester, 1861 England census)

Mad Loony
(Male) Born Alabama *c.*1841
(Hardin, Tennessee, 1860 US census)

John Loopy
Born Ireland *c.*1816
(Tadcaster, Yorkshire, 1841 England census)

Mona Lott
Born Germany *c.*1845 (Galveston, Texas, 1850 US census)

Anton Lunatic
Born Croatia *c.*1888; passenger on *La Touraine*, Le Havre, France–New York, USA, arrived 14 May 1906

George Mad
Married Jane Cole, Cucklington, Somerset, 1 February 1699

Milo Madman
Born Iowa *c.*1895 (Winnebago, Iowa, 1920 US census)

Strange Young Mann
Born Mechanicsburg, Ohio, *c.*1822 (Goshen, Ohio, 1850 US census); married Union, Ohio, 13 December 1866

Anne Constance Misery
Married Jean Baptiste Noel, Paris, France, 23 September 1830

Constance Moan
Born 8 July 1907; died La Crosse, Wisconsin, USA, 29 December 1979

Minnie Moron
Born 8 June 1932; died Fort Worth, Texas, USA, November 1975

Notorious Mosley
Died Chicago, Illinois, USA, 31 December 1986

Babe Mucky
Born Indiana *c.*1869 (Oakwood, Illinois, 1870 US census)

Adolf Nasty
Married Paula Schrodlein, New York, USA, 15 October 1883

Edward Linsher Darby Bright Nerd

Baptized Melcombe Regis, Dorset, 17 December 1806

Absolutely Nobody

Born 7 January 1957; died Seattle, Washington,
USA, 26 October 1993

Harry Nobody

Born c.1901; died Mile End Old Town, London, 1905

Big Nose

Born Colorado c.1850 (Maple, Oklahoma, 1900 US census)

Ima Nutt

Born c.1882 (Shelby, Texas, 1930 US census)

Odious Nutt

Born 17 June 1879; died Navarro, Texas,
USA, 3 September 1965

Dicy Oaf

Born Tennessee c.1844 (Hardin, Tennessee, 1860 US census)

Juan Obese

Born Cuba c.1835; passenger on *City of Vera Cruz*, Havana,
Cuba–New York, USA, arrived 21 July 1876

N. Obrain

Born Ontario c.1857 (Goderich Town,
Ontario, Canada 1871 census)

Ima Pain

Born Georgia 1891 (Clark, Georgia, 1900 US census)

Bernard Pathetic

Died Milwaukee, Wisconsin, USA, 3 October 1880

Stu Pidd
Born Chesterfield, Derbyshire, 1949

Ugly Plug
(Male) Born Washington c.1810
(Lewis, Washington, 1880 US census)

Miserable Porter
(Female) Born c.1913 (Greenville, Alabama, 1930 US census)

Failure Radley
Born Lambeth, London, 1864

Horrible Richel
Born Canada c.1910 (North Attleborough,
Massachusetts, 1930 US census)

Narcissa Rotten
Married John Blackburn, Chambers, Alabama,
USA, 20 December 1849

Robert Rubbish
Born 16 August 1702; baptized St Olave,
Southwark, London, 23 August 1702

Rebecca Rude
Married Nicholas Juell, Holsworthy,
Devon, 10 November 1641

Billy Silly
Baptized Markfield, Leicestershire, 13 September 1603

Wash Slime
Born South Carolina c.1844
(Cooper, South Carolina, 1880 US census)

Fred Slob
Born Iowa *c.*1858 (Orange City, Iowa, 1880 US census)

Sleppy Sloppy
Born Benton, Washington, USA, 6 February 1908

Ima Smelly
Born 14 July 1899; died Suwanee, Georgia, USA, June 1981

Loser Snodgrass
(Male) Born Ohio *c.*1861 (Stokes, Ohio, 1880 US census)

Paul Soggy
Married Mary Cogsequom, Elbridge,
Michigan, USA, 27 May 1895

Bernard Stinker
Born Dinsmore, Ohio, USA, 27 October 1879

Pretty Stout
(Female) Born *c.*1923 (Durham, Kansas, 1930 US census)

Flippin Strange
Born 27 December 1911; died Anawalt,
West Virginia, USA, January 1969

Clarissa Stupid
Born Louisiana *c.*1861 (Lafayette, Indiana, 1880 US census)

Thomas Terrible
Married Hannah Hooper, Stroud,
Gloucestershire, 30 August 1779

John James Thicky
Baptized First and Second Presbyterian Church, New York,
America, 21 September 1766

Mary Drippy Tilley
Married Spalding, Lincolnshire, 1847

Anne Twit
Baptized Carlton Juxta Snaith, Yorkshire, 12 July 1663

Britus Twitty
Born 29 November 1946; died Detroit, Michigan, USA,
13 November 1989

Mary Useless
Born Ireland *c.*1819 (New York, 1870 US census)

Ephraim Uriah Weird
Born South Shields, Durham, 1902

Baldy Wiggins
Born North Carolina 1863
(Griffins, North Carolina, 1900 US census)

Absurd Wilcox
Resident of Denmark Town, New York, USA
(1860 New York census)

Jet Wimp
(Male) Born Illinois 1869 (Dallas, Illinois, 1900 US census)

Phebe Yuck
Baptized Brougham Street Primitive Methodist Chapel, West
Hartlepool, Durham, 20 January 1876

Strange Science

Ida Backup
Born Massachusetts 1850
(Boston, Massachusetts, 1900 US census)

Alice Bell Battery
Born Distington, Cumberland, c.1875
(Distington, 1881 England census)

Barbara Blogger
Born Virginia c.1836 (Alexandria, Virginia, 1860 US census)

William Broadband
Baptized South Leith, Midlothian, 4 October 1660

Dot Com
Born Nebraska c.1887
(Milton, Wisconsin, 1905 Wisconsin, USA, census)

Royal Computer
Born Ballard, Kentucky, USA, 22 February 1911

Mary Cordless
Born Manchester, Lancashire, 1874

Cairo Devontae A. Digital
Born Enfield, Middlesex, 1999

Minnie Disque
Married John Stoll, Hamilton, Ohio, USA, 22 June 1886

Hardy Driver
Born Thornton, Yorkshire, c.1854
(Thornton, 1861 England census)

Henry Ebay
Born Southwark, London, c.1861
(Lambeth, London, 1901 England census)

Ona Email
(Male) Born Colorado c.1907
(Cedar Hill, New Mexico, 1910 US census)

John A. Geek
Born Maryland c.1859
(Hagerstown, Maryland, 1860 US census)

Wanda Gizmo
Born Hardin, Iowa, USA, 1917; died 15 September 1925

Temperantia Google
Baptized Aldborough, Norfolk, 13 August 1598

Email Grist
Born Chichester, Sussex, 1884

Atomic Kane
Married Nancy Wetteland, San Mateo, California,
USA, 26 December 1964

Molly Kewell
Born Westhampnett, Sussex, 1911

Katie Keyboard
Born Ohio 1877 (Franklin, Ohio, 1900 US census)

James Kilowatt
Married Ellen Binninger, Reno, Nevada, USA, 3 July 1974

Abraham Logoff
Born St George in the East, London, 1891

Louisa Logon
Baptized Holy Trinity, Stratford-upon-Avon,
Warwickshire, 26 September 1806

Ann Mobile
Baptized Deddington, Oxfordshire, 21 March 1730

John Online
Born Maryland c.1856 (Baltimore, Maryland, 1870 US census)

Daniel Web Page
Born c.1858; died Benton, Arkansas, USA, 18 July 1943

Henry Home Page
Born Leominster, Herefordshire, c.1873
(Kensington, London, 1901 England census)

I. Phone
Born Romania c.1881 (Bronx, New York, 1920 US census)

I. Pod
(Male) Baptized Whatfield, Suffolk, 20 May 1638

Claude Printout
Born 14 February 1910; died Augusta, Georgia, USA, October 1974

Philip Radar
Born Stepney, London, 1888

X. Ray
Born New York c.1876 (New York, 1880 US census)

Anna Robot
Born Germany c.1821
(St George's Hanover Square, London, 1851 England census)
The word 'robot' was invented by Czech writer Karel Capek in his play R.U.R. (Rossum's Universal Robots) *(1920), which was translated into English in 1928.*

C. D. Rom
Born Kenton, Kentucky, USA, 25 July 1972

Abraham Scanner
Born July Ann Bingder, Conway,
Michigan, USA, 15 March 1905

My Space
Born Idaho c.1903 (Pierce, Idaho, 1910 US census)
Myron Space, the son of Christian and Ida Space, was known in his family as 'My'.

Minnie Spam
Born 7 December 1912; died Flushing,
New York, USA, 4 March 2002

Thomas Text
Born Bourne, Lincolnshire, 1887

Tom Tom
Born Bristol, Gloucestershire, c.1862
(Barton Regis, Gloucestershire, 1891 England census)

Anna Tomic
Born 26 June 1895; died Ironwood,
Michigan, USA, April 1979

Thomas Twitter
Born Wigan, Lancashire, 1861

Ida Virus
Born 18 April 1909; died Hebron,
Nebraska, USA, September 1985

W. W. Web
Born Georgia c.1845
(Baker, Georgia, 1850 US census)

Augusta Website
Born Germany c.1865
(Grandview, Illinois, 1870 US census)

Leah Wifi
Born UK c.1854; passenger on *Britannic*, Liverpool,
UK–New York, USA, arrived 14 April 1884

Mike Wireless
Born Germany c.1868
(Baltimore, Maryland, 1880 US census)

EXOTIC ELEMENTS

●●●●●●●●●●●●●●●●

Delta Molybdenum Abbott
Born Wandsworth, London, 2000

Arsenic Borwoski
Born New York, USA, 30 October 1895

Chromium Brown
Born Hull, Yorkshire, 1984

Barium Butler
(Female) Born Louisiana c.1854
(East Feliciana, Louisiana, 1870 US census)

Truly Carbon
Born Dorking, Surrey, c.1869
(Broadwater Down, Kent, 1901 England census)

Calcium Carter
(Female) Born Virginia 1846
(Wicomico, Virginia, 1900 US census)

Neon Chance
(Female) Born 1874 (Sandoval, Illinois, 1900 US census)

Sulphur Cole
(Male) Born Georgia c.1866 (Bryan, Georgia, 1870 US census)

Iodine Coward
Born Georgia c.1868 (Charlton, Georgia, 1870 US census)

Chlorine Daily
(Female) Born 24 October 1909; died Aquilla,
Texas, USA, 16 October 1981

Eleanor Element
Baptized Orleton, Herefordshire, 2 November 1823

Argon Fax
(Male) Born c.1915 (Roseville, Michigan, 1930 US census)

Cobalt Flannely
Born Ireland c.1800 (Washington, DC, 1860 US census)

Rose Germanium
Born Kingsland, London, c.1875
(Hackney, London, 1891 England census)

Agnes Silver Gold
Born c.1870; died Wigan, Lancashire, 1910

Alumina Goldberger
(Female) Born Tennessee c.1891
(Memphis, Tennessee, 1910 US census)

Copper Horsey
Born Islington, London, 1856

Arthur Phosphor Mallam
Born Headington, Oxfordshire, 1872

Constant Manganese
Born 15 August 1920; died Boston,
Massachusetts, USA, 25 January 1993

Helium McKinney
Born Mississippi c.1875 (Monroe, Arkansas, 1920 US census)

Bromine Parks
(Male) Born Indiana c.1854
(Marshall, Indiana, 1920 US census)

Thomas Nickel Penny
Died Kendal, Cumbria, 1849

Fluorine R. Pickelheimer
Born 5 May 1917; died Cincinnati, Ohio, USA, 4 March 2002

Element Reid
(Male) Born Wheathampstead, Hertfordshire, 10 July 1821

Silicon Rubidoux
Born South Dakota c.1879
(Meyer, South Dakota, 1900 US census)

Antimony Scott
(Female) Born Virginia c.1866
(Greene, Tennessee, 1880 US census)

Radon Skinner
Born 27 November 1979; died
Dallas, Texas, USA, 16 June 1996

Oxygen Smith
Born 11 August 1937; died New York, USA, 16 May 2008

Radium Stanley
Born Arkansas 26 June 1911; died San Joaquin,
California, USA, 30 August 1982

Armor Tungsten Steele
Born 29 May 1916; died San Joaquin,
California, USA, 4 August 1997

Lithium Stinger
(Female) Born Indiana c.1825
(Wayne, Indiana, 1850 US census)

Phosphorus Stone
Married Stepney, London, 1866

Boron Tanner
Born Coventry, Warwickshire, 1879

Platinum Che'yrael Townsend
Born Lewisham, London, 2002

Gladys Xenon Watkins
Born West Ham, Essex, 1899

Zinc White
Born 28 August 1873; died Oakland,
Mississippi, USA, October 1968

Eli Uranium Wiggins
Born Nash, North Carolina, USA, 12 April 1948

ASTOUNDING ASTRONOMY
● ●

Mercury Devall
(Female) Born Redhill, Surrey, c.1898
(Chipstead, Surrey, 1901 England census)

Mars and Venus Neptune
Twins, born Wyoming, USA, 16 March 1897

Earth Stone
(Female) Baptized Deptford, Kent, 3 August 1718

Jupiter Battle
Born 24 November 1899; died Detroit,
Michigan, USA, May 1965

Saturn Vega
Born 29 March 1923; died Los Angeles,
California, USA, 12 March 1981

Uranus Wild
(Male) Born North Carolina c.1879
(Warm Springs, North Carolina, 1880 US census)

Neptune Skidmore
Died New York, USA, 15 July 1902

Pluto Matthews
Born Florida c.1930 (Lake, 1935 Florida, USA, census)
*Pluto Matthews was born in the year that
Pluto was discovered by American
astronomer Clyde Tombaugh.*

Evelina Asteroid
Born Louisiana 1880
(New Orleans, Louisiana, 1880 US census)

Leonides Astronomo
Born Nagcarian, Philippines, 15 September 1947;
died Nagcarian 16 July 1996

Orion Belt
Born 23 March 1922; died New Windsor,
Maryland, USA, 6 March 2006

Galaxy Craze
Born Hammersmith, London, 1970

Quasar Freedom Dopler
(Male) Born Lubock, Texas, USA,
3 November 1975

Illuminada Eclipse

Born 27 May 1918; died Jamaica,
New York, USA, 16 April 1999

Doran Equinox

Born 22 September 1969; died Oakland,
California, USA, 1 June 2001

Comet Halley

(Male) Born Michigan 10 July 1910; died Muskegon,
Michigan, USA, 2 January 1976

Universe Duchess Hambayi

Born 2 September 1944; died Hillingdon,
Middlesex, February 2005

Halley Comet Jones

Born Marion, Texas, USA, 19 May 1910
*Halley's Comet was visible from
Earth in the month Halley was born.*

Planet Jones

(Female) Born Breconshire c.1839
(Lower Ystradgynlais, 1841 Wales census)

Meteor Lafleur

Born 6 October 1912; died Kinder,
Texas, USA, 7 January 1990

Star Light

Born 12 August 1912; died New York, USA, January 1980

Galaxy Lloye

Married John Moreland, Frederick,
Virginia, USA, 18 April 1822

Moon Manly

(Male) Born *c*.1863 (Independence,
Kansas, USA, 1905 Kansas census)

Honey Moon

(Male) Born Wisconsin *c*.1903
(Campbell, California, 1910 US census)

Sun Moon

Born 23 July 1920; died Los Angeles,
California, USA, 28 November 1992

Joseph Nebula

Born Italy *c*.1882 (Young, Pennsylvania, 1910 US census)

William Orbit

Born Westminster, London, *c*.1820
(Westminster, 1881 England census)

Abba Planet

Born 9 October 1896; died Kansas City,
Missouri, USA, March 1976

Betty Proton

Baptized Sundon, Bedfordshire, 30 April 1731

Phinlo Quark

Baptized Lonan, Isle of Man, 20 March 1723

Planet Smiler

(Male) Born Georgia 1890 (Bainbridge,
Georgia, 1900 US census)

Eclipse Sutton

Born 25 July 1911; died Detroit,
Michigan, USA, 8 April 1991

NUTTY NUMBERS

Zero Pie
(Male) Born c.1913 (Franks, Arkansas, 1930 US census)
Zero was the son of Pearlie Pie and brother of Loveanna Pie.

Vera Zero
Born 8 June 1914; died Brooklyn, New York,
USA, 27 February 2006

William No. 1 Harris
Married Islington, London, 1896

William No. 2 Harris
Married Maria A. Trent, Islington, London, 1913

Harry Two Smith
Married Derby 1900

Three Worthy
Born 1 June 1907; died Linden, Alabama, USA, April 1981

Four Souls
Born 16 April 1907; died Box Elder, Montana, USA, July 1984

Five Bumball
(Female) Born Pennsylvania c.1840
(Jackson, Missouri, 1920 US census)

Six Hix
(Female) Born South Carolina c.1898
(Waterloo, South Carolina, 1910 US census)

Number Seven Fell
Born Alton, Hampshire, 1879

Eight McClurg
(Female) Born Iowa *c.*1879
(White Breast, Iowa, 1880 US census)

Nine Sparks
Born 18 July 1939; died Jackson,
Montana, USA, 25 August 1995

Ten Hipkiss
Born Birmingham, Warwickshire, *c.*1898
(Birmingham, 1911 England census)

Eleven Moore
Born 11 July 1900; died Coalgate,
Oklahoma, USA, January 1982

Twelve Ripley
(Female) Born Illinois 1887 (Ora, Illinois, 1900 US census)

Thirteen R. Murillo
Born 18 April 1928; died New Rochelle,
New York, USA, 13 June 2005

Fourteen E. Falconer
Married Clyde M. Wright, Milton Keynes,
Buckinghamshire, 1986

Twenty Man Hodgson
Born Whitehaven, Cumberland, *c.*1828
(Whitehaven, 1881 England census)

Luke Twenty-One Chretien
Born Kings Lynn, Norfolk, 1978

Thirty Wilson
(Female) Born Tennessee *c.*1879
(Henry, Tennessee, 1880 US census)

Forty Weieze
Born Germany c.1858 (Willesden,
Middlesex, 1901 England census)

Fifty Townsend
(Male) Born Alabama c.1877
(Montgomery, Alabama, 1920 US census)

Fifty Six Richardson
Born Alabama c.1869 (Gainesville, Alabama, 1870 US census)

Tom Fifty Nine Coates
Born Darlington, Durham, c.1876
(Darlington, 1881 England census)

Sixty Moore
Born 1 July 1881; died Alaska, USA, December 1963

Seventy Head
Born 24 March 1897; died Pinellas, Florida, USA, July 1964

Eighty Coonrod
Born South Carolina c.1843
(York, South Carolina, 1870 US census)

Ninety Griffin
Born 19 April 1908; died Apple Springs,
Texas, USA, December 1980

Hundred Evans
Died Greene, Alabama, USA, 1 January 1949

Thousand Poindexter
Born Louisiana c.1888 (Gibson, Louisiana, 1920 US census)

Million Airth
(Female) Born Ontario, Canada, 4 June 1869

Ivor Million
Born Salford, Lancashire, 1928

Ten Million
Born 14 October 1889; died Washington, USA, June 1964

Billion Pride
(Male) Born c.1898 (Brooklyn, New York, 1930 US census)
A billion is a thousand million – a one followed by nine zeros.

Milliard Body
(Female) Born Birmingham, Warwickshire, c.1898
(Aston, Warwickshire, 1901 England census)
A milliard is another word for a billion.

Trillion Cummings
(Female) Born Mississippi c.1907
(Kirkville, Mississippi, 1910 US census)
A trillion is a million million – a one followed by 12 zeros.

Zillion Long
Born 15 March 1899; died Petersburg,
Virginia, USA, October 1977
*Along with words such as squillion and gazillion,
there is no such number as a zillion, but it is sometimes
used to mean a very large number.*

Infinity Hubbard
(Female) Born Georgia c.1839
(Tipah, Mississippi, 1850 US census)

Minnie Fraction
Born 31 January 1890; died Memphis, Tennessee, USA, March 1982

Decimal Jones
Born Corwen, Denbighshire, 1889

WACKY WEATHER

•••••••••••••••

Lot Blizzard
Baptized Great Somerford,
Wiltshire, 30 November 1794

George Snowdrift Bone
Born St Saviour, Southwark, London, 1881

Freezer Breeze
(Female) Born Great Yarmouth, Norfolk, *c*.1839
(Great Yarmouth, 1851 England census)

Ada I. Cicle
Born *c*.1865 (Elm Grove, Oklahoma, 1930 US census)

Helen Climate
Baptized Morton by Thornhill, Dumfries, 13 September 1730

Icicle Star Crumplin
Born Hampshire 2002

Snow Shovel Curley
(Female) Born Oklahoma *c*.1890
(Lincoln, Oklahoma, 1900 US census)

John Cyclone
Born Indiana *c*.1875 (Tippecanoe, Indiana, 1920 US census)

A. Lovely Day
Born Alaska 17 October 1895;
died Los Angeles, California, USA, 14 March 1986

Raini Day
Born West Virginia 12 August 1962;
died Ohio, USA, 21 January 2002

Sunny Day
(Male) Born Maryland c.1865
(Westover, Maryland, 1910 US census)

Winter Day
Born Romsey, Hampshire, 1845

Priscilla Drizzle
Born 30 March 1911; died Detroit, Michigan, 15 April 1999

Hurricane Du Gay
Born Switzerland c.1863 (Camberwell,
London, 1911 England census)

Experience Fairweather
Resident of Newport, Rhode Island (1840 US census)

Eva Foggy
Born 1902; died Charleston,
South Carolina, USA, 13 October 1927

Gale Force
Born c.1925 (Navy Yard, Kitsap, Washington, 1930 US census)

Freak Frost
(Male) Born Dagenham, Essex, c.1864
(Lewisham, London, 1901 England census)

Icie Snow Frost
(Female) Born Ohio c.1869 (Harrison, Ohio, 1880 US census)

Lenora I. C. Frost
Born Medway, Kent, 1924

Winter Frost
(Male) Born Kidderminster, Worcestershire, 1859

Isabella Blows Gale
Born Greenwich, Kent, 1837

Dewey Grass
Born North Carolina 1899
(Knobs, North Carolina, 1900 US census)

Drizzle Hagin
Married Simon Henry, Oktibbeha, Mississippi,
USA, 7 November 1874

Blooming Ice
(Male) Born Alabama c.1852
(Marshall, Alabama, 1860 US census)

Esonon Isobar
(Female) Baptized Irstead, Norfolk, May 1569
*An isobar is a line on a weather map connecting places
of equal barometric pressure.*

Esau Lightning
Married Emily Potter, Aslacton, Norfolk, 14 June 1836

Lavinah Mist
Baptized Ellingham, Hampshire, 24 June 1833

Cloudy Night
(Female) Born North Carolina c.1915
(Hectors Creek, North Carolina, 1920 US census)

Snowflake George Pledger
Born Hampstead, London, 1877

Frozen Prince
Born Canada c.1864 (St Albans, Vermont, 1880 US census)

Minnie Raindrop
Born 1888 (Magnolia, South Carolina, 1900 US census)

Les Rainey
Born Texas c.1863
(Fincastle, Texas, 1880 US census)

Neva Rains
Born Oklahoma c.1914
(Pomona, California, 1930 US census)

Hiram Brown Rainwater
Born St Merryn, Cornwall, 9 October 1881

Gusty Sandbag
Born c.1853; died Thornbury, Gloucestershire, 1902

Roosevelt Seabreeze
Born 24 May 1937; died Nashville, North Carolina,
USA, 19 June 2004

April Showers
Born 27 February 1956; died Wilmington,
California, USA, 16 May 2008

Gale Showers
Born 4 April 1911; died Avoca, Iowa,
USA, 19 December 2000

Gale Sunshine Showers
Married James Woodham, Pasco,
Florida, USA, April 1965

Abraham Sleet
Married Sarah Tayler, Hemel Hempstead,
Hertfordshire, 8 May 1700

Utan Smog
(Male) Born Kentucky c.1823
(Assumption, Louisiana, 1880 US census)

Early Snow
Born Surry, North Carolina, USA, 4 March 1893

Zebier Snowball Snowball
Born Nottingham 2004

East Snowdrift
Born Bienville, Louisiana, c.1812
(Bienville, 1880 US census)

Breezy Stoneburner
Born 23 May 1906; died San Diego,
California, USA, 5 September 1993

Silence Storm
Born 22 March 1898; died Peoria,
Illinois, USA, May 1982

Rainbow Sunshine
Born 5 March 1892; died New York, USA, April 1979

Hannah Velocity Tempest
Born c.1834; died Shoreditch, London, 1886

Rufino Tornado
Married Trinidad Fernands, Inmaculada Concepcion,
Villa Cordoba, Argentina, 22 October 1818

Martha Snowflake Tozer
Born Holywell, Flintshire, 21 January 1892

Pleasant Weathers
(Male) Born Mississippi c.1858
(Leake, Mississippi, 1860 US census)

Enoch Wildgust
Married Sarah Atkin, St Peter's,
Nottingham, 11 November 1860

Agusta Wind
Born Prussia c.1850 (Hurricane, Illinois, 1880 US census)
Note the name of town she lived in!

Hy Wind
Born Bethnal Green, London, c.1865
(Poplar, London, 1871 England census)

Theophilus Windy
Born Weston, Lincolnshire, c.1823
(Weston, 1901 England census)

Ernest Frosty Winter
Born Leeds, Yorkshire, 1878

Walter Spring Winter
Born Romford, Essex, 1885

Ocean Storm Wise
Born Exeter, Devon, 2002

Curious Creatures and Puzzling Plants

CURIOUS CREATURES

Koala Ah
Resident of Wailuku, Hawaii (1910 Hawaii census)

Minnie Aligator [*sic*]
Born New York 1890 (Brooklyn, New York, 1900 US census)

Baboon Dalbert Anson
(Female) Born Scotland c.1844
(Clewer, Berkshire, 1871 England census)

Ann Ant
Born Wadena, Minnesota, USA, 3 September 1893;
died Minneapolis, Minnesota, July 1982

Abraham Ape
Baptized Staindrop, Durham, 4 January 1669

Liz Ard
Born Ireland c.1824 (Waltham Abbey,
Essex, 1871 England census)

Hamster C. Armatys
(Male) Born Clerkenwell, London, c.1853
(Headingley, Yorkshire, 1901 England census)

Grasshopper Arrowsmith

(Female) Born Kansas c.1875
(Geneva, Nebraska, 1880 US census)

Jack Ass

Born 24 April 1958; died Hot Springs,
Montana, USA, 21 July 2003

Paulina Baboon

Born Augusta, Kennebec, Maine,
USA, 25 June 1806; died 12 April 1883

Diehappy Badger

(Female) Born West Bromwich, Staffordshire, c.1860
(West Bromwich, 1861 England census)

Ima Badger

Born 12 August 1934; died Woodland,
California, USA, 9 February 2008

Minty Badger

Married Southam, Warwickshire, 1866

Smiley Badger

(Female) Born Napton, Warwickshire
(Southam, Warwickshire, 1901 England census)

Mary Balamb

Born c.1811 (St Giles-in-the-Fields,
London, 1841 England census)

Chicken Barber

(Male) Born Alabama c.1879
(Midway, Alabama, 1880 US census)

Cat Basket
Married Robert Girling, St Matthew's,
Ipswich, Suffolk, 19 November 1764

Ruth Trout Bass
Born Tennessee c.1897 (Richmond, Virginia, 1920 US census)

Basil Bat
Baptized Aydius, France, 12 February 1799

Henry Savage Bear
Born c.1802; died Medway, Kent, 1873

Mathew Foolish Bear
Born 30 November 1939; died New Town,
North Dakota, 8 June 2003

Benjamin Beast
Married Mary Earle, Buxted, Sussex, 16 February 1674

Pinky Beavers
Born 24 February 1887 (Blount, Alabama,
USA, First World War draft registration)

Bea Bee
Born Windsor, Berkshire, 1866

Large Bee
(Male) Born Nottinghamshire c.1829
(Nottingham, 1891 England census)
His son was also called Large Bee.

May Bee
Married James Rowlands, Scarborough, Yorkshire, 1922

Unique Keanu S. Bee
Born Nottingham 2002

Elephant Bill
(Male) Born California c.1821
(Fresno, California, 1860 US census)

Ladybird Bingley
Born Kensington, London, 1871

Dangerous Bird
Born c.1879 (Montana, 1891 US Indian census)

Dicky Bird
Born Edmonton, Middlesex, 1894

Early Bird
Married Phillips Harris, Colbert,
Alabama, USA, 4 December 1881

Ima Bird
Born Iowa c.1887 (Ouachita, Arkansas, 1910 US census)

Luscious Bird
(Male) Born Kentucky c.1889
(Allen, Kentucky, 1910 US census)

Tiny Bird
(Female) Born Texas c.1876 (Melrose, Texas, 1880 US census)

Locust Blood
(Male) Born New York c.1916 (New York, 1920 US census)

Creature Bonner
Baptized St Botolph Bishopsgate, London, 8 January 1643

Bobcat Bruce
Born Leslie, Fifeshire, c.1813
(Strathmiglo, Fifeshire, 1871 Scotland census)

Margerie Budgie
Married William Coles, Solihull,
Warwickshire, 9 February 1571

Ura Buffalo
Born 5 April 1909; died Jacksonville,
Texas, USA, 17 June 1994

Elmo Bugg
Born 24 September 1904; died Los Angeles,
California, USA, February 1980

Ferrel Bugg
Born 25 November 1881; died Greensboro,
North Carolina, USA, November 1975

Saint Bugg
Died Bourne, Lincolnshire, 1840
'Saint' was his first name.

Slaughter Bugg
Born Louisiana *c*.1891
(Pointe Coupee, Louisiana, 1930 US census)

Tiny Bugg
(Female) Born Georgia 1835 (Askew,
Georgia, 1900 US census)

Odd Bugge
Born Norway *c*.1929; crew on *Reinholt*, Baltimore,
Maryland–New York, USA, arrived 30 July 1948

Bad Heart Bull
US Army enlistment, 12 January 1891

Fart Bull
(Male) Born c.1851 (Montana, 1885 US Indian census)

Angeline Bumblebee
Married Frank McDonald, Cheboygan,
Michigan, USA, 17 December 1879

Arthur Bumblebee
Died Summit, Ohio, USA, 4 January 1922

William Mole Burrow
Born Wellingborough, Northamptonshire, 1853

Camel Camel
Baptized St Peter and St Kevin,
Dublin, Ireland, 9 August 1733

Mixwater Chicken
Born 1 December 1932; died Oklahoma, USA, May 1973

Rose Chicken
Born Sunderland, Durham, 1927

Richard Chimp
Married Anne Wells, St Albans Abbey,
Hertfordshire, 22 April 1679

Ann Chovey
Born France *c.*1810 (Fort Wayne, Indiana, 1880 US census)

Francesca Coconut Coby
Born Oxford 1994

Anna Conder
Born Mile End, London, *c.*1794
(West Ham, Essex, 1851 England census)

Gorilla Cook
(Female) Born Georgia *c.*1867
(Milltown, Georgia, 1910 US census)

Nippy Goose Craig
(Female) Born Scotland *c.*1885
(Fulham, London, 1911 England census)
*Nippy's profession, as listed in the 1911
census, was 'comedian'.*

Mungo Creature
Baptized Holm and Paplay, Orkney, 2 April 1769

Ebenezer Hedgehog T. Cringebottom
Born Mendip, Somerset, 1990

Jane Crocodile
Born *c.*1822 (Blandford, Dorset, 1841 England census)

Nightingale Cuckoo
Died Westminster, London, 1838

Camel Dancer
Born 8 April 1930; died Cincinnati,
Ohio, USA, 10 October 1978

Jack Daw
Born Bermondsey, London, c.1872
(Bermondsey, 1901 England census)

Elizabeth Dodo
Baptized Bristol, Gloucestershire, 12 July 1738

Cat Dog
Baptized Dundee, Angus, 13 November 1679

Donnie L. Ghost Dog
Born 11 March 1971; died South Dakota,
USA, 14 November 2000

Iona Dolphin
Born 13 June 1905; died Burlington,
Vermont, USA, January 1990

Zephaniah Donkey
Baptized St Peter's, Liverpool, Lancashire, 2 April 1827

Lovey Dove
(Male) Born Georgia c.1908
(Franklin, Georgia, 1910 US census)

Peace Dove
Baptized Bourne, Lincolnshire, 9 November 1668

Fairy Duck
Born c.1894 (Harvey, Illinois, 1930 US census)

Fart Duck
(Male) Born c.1881 (Colorado River,
Arizona Territory, 1889 US Indian census)

King Duck
Born Alabama c.1873 (Union Springs,
Alabama, 1880 US census)

Lovey Duck
Born Mississippi c.1825 (Amite, Mississippi, 1880 US census)

Rhoda Duck
Born Guisborough, Yorkshire, 1905

Wildcat Duke
Born Alabama c.1870 (Monroe, Alabama, 1870 US census)

Fart Eagle
(Male) Born c.1849 (South Dakota, 1893 US Indian census)

Sarah Earwig
Married James Arrow, East Ham, Essex, 28 March 1810

Pincus Elephant
Born Russia c.1886 (New York, 1910 US census)

Ellie Fant
Born c.1927 (Newberry, South Carolina, 1930 US census)

Baby Weasel Fat
Born Alberta c.1882 (Alberta, 1916 census of
Manitoba, Saskatchewan and Alberta, Canada)

Mary Ann Fieldmouse
Married Wolverhampton, Staffordshire, 1877

Fish Fish
Born Salford, Lancashire, 1840

Happy Fish
Died Wangford, Suffolk, 1837

Preserved Fish
Born Portsmouth, Rhode Island, America, 16 March 1677;
died Portsmouth 15 July 1744
There were several people called Preserved Fish in America –
another (born 14 July 1766, died 23 July 1846) was a
well-known merchant in New York.

Mary Stoat O. Float
Born Plymouth, Devon, *c.*1828
(Plymouth, 1851 England census)

Alien Fly
Born 4 May 1902; died Jackson, Tennessee, USA, 1 June 1994

Burpee Fox
Born Alexander, North Carolina, USA, 31 December 1915

Cheerful Fox
Born 11 August 1925; died Canonsburg,
Pennsylvania, USA, 5 October 2000

Foxy Fox
(Male) Born 1947; died Bangor, Caernarvonshire, 1999

Ima Fox
Born Texas 1894 (Bowie, Texas, 1900 US census)

Wolf Fox
Born Whitechapel, London, *c.*1876
(Whitechapel, 1881 England census)

Charlie Wooden Frog
Born c.1898 (St Louis, Minnesota, 1930 US census)

Pearlie Frogge
Born 20 December 1884; died St Joseph,
Missouri, USA, August 1973

Kangaroo Fuller
Died Dallas, Texas, USA, 23 January 1963

Oyster Gamble
Born 28 April 1919; died Williamsburg,
South Carolina, USA, July 1981

Mamie Gerbil
Born Georgia c.1876 (Atlanta, Georgia, 1930 US census)

Nancy Goat
Born Tennessee 1880 (Savannah, Tennessee, 1900 US census)

Frank Gorilla
Born Michigan c.1901 (Gogebic, Michigan, 1910 US census)

Sage Gorilla
(Female) Born Breitung Township,
Michigan, USA, 19 June 1885

Timothy Goosehead
Born Manitoba, c.1886 (Selkirk,
Manitoba, 1911 Canada census)

Mary Grasshopper
Baptized St Giles without Cripplegate,
London, 7 February 1762

Albatross Grayson
(Male) Born 14 March 1905; died Stanislaus,
Texas, USA, 3 February 1983

John Hamster
Married Elizabeth Pearson, Sheffield Cathedral,
Sheffield, Yorkshire, 2 February 1784

Turtledove Hancock
Married Daniel Warden, St Martin-in-the-Fields, London, 1795

Spider Harness
Born c.1833 (Hancock, Illinois, 1860 US census)

Hippo Hatcher
(Male) Born c.1919 (Hayneville, Alabama, 1930 US census)

Marjorie Wild Goose Hayre
Born Stamford, Lincolnshire, c.1907
(Stamford, 1911 England census)
*Marjorie and her younger sister Greta were both
given the middle names 'Wild Goose'.*

Charity Hedgehog
Born c.1780, Caswell, North Carolina, USA; married James
Langley, Caswell, North Carolina, USA, 1810;
died Lee, Virginia, 1850

Priscilla Hippo
Baptized St Matthew's, Bethnal Green, London,
13 October 1782

Holly Hock
Born Wisconsin c.1890 (Waukesha, Wisconsin, 1920 US census)

Ima Hogg

Born 10 July 1882; died Houston, Texas, USA, 19 August 1975

Ima Hogg was the daughter of James Hogg, the Governor of Texas. Her grandfather complained about her name, but too late – she had already been baptized. When she grew up, she signed her name so no one could read it properly. Some people claim she had a sister called Ura Hogg, but this is not true.

Herring Hooks

Born Georgia *c.*1824 (Americus, Georgia, 1870 US census)

Birdie Trail Hospital

Died Lee, Florida, USA, February 1964

Giraffe House

Died Jefferson, Alabama, USA, 28 August 1917

Python Howsam

Born Pontesbury, Shropshire, *c.*1900
(Pontesbury, 1901 England census)

Mustafa Kamel

Born Egypt *c.*1892; passenger on *Homeric*,
Southampton, UK–New York, USA, arrived 9 July 1924

Quorum Scorpion B. Kevan

Born Kensington and Chelsea, London, 1996

Hamster King

(Female) Born *c.*1771; died Charleston,
South Carolina, USA, 1833

Emu Kingdom

Born Neath, Glamorgan, 1878

Cat Kitten
Born Lawhitton, Cornwall, *c.*1820
(Launceston, Cornwall, 1851 England census)

Abraham Kiwi
Born New York, USA, 8 November 1872

Zebra Leek
Died Birmingham, Warwickshire, 1865

Minnie Lobster
Born Mississippi *c.*1919 (Carroll, Mississippi, 1920 US census)

Mary Manymules
Born 16 October 1935; died Page,
Arizona, USA, 21 May 2005

Butterfly McQueen
Born 8 January 1911; died New York,
USA, 22 December 1995

Henry Mole Mole
Born Tynemouth, Northumberland, 1867

Clementina Monkey
Baptized Christ Church, Barbados, 23 June 1833

Toad Moon
Born 10 October 1887; died Athens,
Georgia, USA, 29 August 1986

Beveridge Moose
Born 24 December 1929; died Stony Point,
North Carolina, USA, 27 July 1993

Big Mosquito
Born Oklahoma *c*.1850 (Oklahoma, 1900 US census)

Henrietta Mosquito
Born *c*.1884; died Toxteth Park, Lancashire, 1914

Fay Mouse
Born Kentucky *c*.1906 (Liberty, Kentucky, 1920 US census)

Pelican Nelson
(Male) Born New York *c*.1870 (New York 1870 US census)

Armadillo Newman
Born 19 April 1894; died Fulton, Georgia,
USA, 10 August 1971

Puffin Annabelinda O'Hanlon
Born Oxford 1985

Maudlin Orang
Married Isaac Lepley, St Dunstan's, Stepney,
London, 28 February 1700

Polly Parrot
Born England *c*.1830 (Brooklyn, New York, 1880 US census)

Millie Peed
Died Laurmie Township, Indiana, USA, 10 December 1912

Philomena Mary Pelican
Born 7 April 1920; died Hounslow, London, 1988

George Strangeways Pigg
Born Orsett, Essex, 1906

Ima Pigg
Born c.1890 (Erick, Oklahoma, 1930 US census)

Iva Piggee
Born Arkansas c.1891 (Nashville, Arkansas, 1920 US census)

Wiggy Piggy
(Male) Born Virginia c.1878
(Richmond, Virginia, 1880 US census)

Rena Piglet
Born Adair, Kentucky, USA, 1 January 1923

Barney Pigsty
Born Ireland c.1828 (Louisville, Kentucky, 1850 US census)

Ostrich Pockinghorn
Married St Stephen-by-Saltash, Cornwall, 1792

Rich Poodle
Married Lydia Carpenter, Shipton-under-Wychwood,
Oxfordshire, 1836

Ellen Sarah Andrasa Prawn Prawn
Born Newcastle upon Tyne, Northumberland, 1858

Margaret Pussyfoot
Born Victoria, Australia, 1878

Chicken Quamephone
Born 1 July 1888; died Zuni,
New Mexico, USA, 15 January 1967

G. Raffe
Born 10 June 1896; died Chicago, Illinois, USA, February 1975

Annie Rhino
Married Merthyr Tydfil, Glamorgan, 1881

Mike Robe
Baptized Kilsyth, Stirling, 15 May 1743

Dinah Saw
Baptized St Lawrence, Chobham, Surrey, 18 October 1818

Henrietta Shark
Born Sutton, Kent, c.1835
(Camberwell, London, 1851 England census)

Walter Shrimp
Born 12 May 1892; died Sonestown,
Pennsylvania, USA, April 1983

Abraham Singhorse
Citizen of Washington, Pennsylvania (1790 US census)

Sarah Slug
Married Roger Hill, Westbury, Wiltshire, 10 April 1757

Gorilla Small
(Male) Born Georgia 1894
(Gloerville, Georgia, 1900 US census)

Cuckoo Smith
Born Brimpton, Berkshire, c.1877
. (Brimpton, 1881 England census)

Fluffy Bird Smith
(Female) Born Mississippi 1899
(Wilkinson, Mississippi, 1900 US census)

Frank Walrus Smith
Born Portsea Island, Hampshire, 1880

Mice Smith
(Female) Born Cradley, Herefordshire, c.1867 (Suckley, Worcestershire, 1871 England census)

Joseph Squid
Born St George in the East, London, c.1864 (Bethnal Green, London, 1881 England census)

Chevallier Sinbad W. Squirrell [sic]
Born Hatfield, Hertfordshire, 1993

Aligator [sic] Stagg
(Female) Born Mississippi 1878
(Claiborne, Mississippi, 1900 US census)

Bea Sting
Born c.1905 (Manchester, New Hampshire, 1930 US census)

Thomas Stingray
Married Abbie Ponifry, Butler, Alabama, USA, 27 June 1875

Faithfull Tadpole
Baptized St John the Evangelist, Dublin, Ireland, 11 November 1665

Ann Teater
Born Lamberhurst, Sussex, c.1854
(Tonbridge, Kent, 1881 England census)

Thomas Tiger
Married Elizabeth Stout, St Mary's, Beverley, Yorkshire, 23 December 1694

Little Tigertail
Born 19 April 1919; died Clewiston, Florida, USA, 28 June 2003

Jemima Tortoise
Baptized Swafield, Norfolk, 6 April 1794

Loyal Trout
(Male) Born New Jersey, USA, 9 February 1908;
died 13 February 1991

Lancelot Chicken Tulip
Born Chorlton, Lancashire, 1878

Zane Dinosaur Vicknair
Married Vanessa Marie Vicknair, Clark, Nevada, 16 July 2001

Rosetta Viper
Born Bishops Stortford, Hertfordshire, 1862

Spider G. Vonkersburg
Born 2 February 1956; died Cambridge,
Massachusetts, USA, 29 March 2003

Pig Walker
(Male) Born Texas c.1860 (Camp, Texas, 1880 US census)

Trout Walker
Born c.1921 (Cleveland, Ohio, 1930 US census)

Elizabeth Wallaby
Baptized Spennithorne, Yorkshire, 7 March 1780

William Walrus
Born South Dakota 1883
(Brinnon, Washington, 1900 US census)

Bunny Warren
Born 20 April 1911; died Dacorum, Hertfordshire, July 1998

Noble Wasp
Baptized St Mary at Coslany, Norwich,
Norfolk, 27 February 1773

Alice Weasel
Born Poplar, London, 1880

George Weaselboy
Born 20 November 1907; died Box Hill,
Montana, USA, November 1983

Prince Charles Whales
Born Mitford, Norfolk, 1899
'Prince Charles' were his first and middle names.

Gaynwawpiahsika Thomas Alford Wildcat
Born Canadian River, Oklahoma, 15 July 1860;
died Shawnee, Oklahoma, USA, 3 August 1938

Squirrel Wildcat
Born 7 April 1899; died Gore, Oklahoma,
USA, 26 August 1988

Wolf Wolf
Born St George in the East, London, 1886

Alice Zebra
Married Westminster, London, 1864

PUZZLING PLANTS
• • • • • • • • • • • • • • •

Charles Bamboo Africa
Baptized Westminster, London, 6 May 1815

Hazel Twig

Born Indiana c.1901 (Wabash, Indiana, 1910 US census)

Buttercup Bazalgette

Born Hull, Yorkshire, c.1888 (Wimbledon,
1901 England census)

Lolita Beanblossom

Born c.1925 (Burr Oak, Jewell, Kansas, 1930 US census)

Olive Branch

Born West Ham, Essex, 1880

Myrtle Branch

Born Illinois c.1899 (Salem, Illinois, 1910 US census)

Rose Bud

Born Pennsylvania c.1841 (Marietta,
Pennsylvania, 1860 US census)

Ima Rose Bush

Born New York c.1904 (Osceola, Michigan, 1910 US census)

Earthland Cabbagestalk

(Male) Born South Carolina c.1915 (Mechanicsville, South
Carolina, 1920 US census)

Pansy Blossom

Born Illinois c.1896 (Macon, Illinois, 1910 US census)

Ellen Cactus

Baptized Northrepps, Norfolk, 31 October 1841

Daisy Chain

Born Kansas c.1886 (Dallas, Texas, 1920 US census)

Mourning Chesnut [*sic*]
Resident of Sampson, North Carolina (1790 US census)

Daisy Forget-me-not Crouch
Born Brentford, Middlesex, 1888

Leafy Forest
(Female) Born Kansas c.1906 (Lauray, Kansas, 1920 US census)

Ever Green
Born Lexden, Essex, 1847

Theresa Green
Baptized Motcombe, Dorset, 23 September 1804

Vine Leaf
Born York 1896

Dan D. Lyons
Born Cardiff, Glamorgan, 1891 (Cardiff, 1891 Wales census)

Savage Nettles
Born 3 March 1906; died Paramount,
California, USA, 27 March 2000

Forest Nutgrass
Born Kentucky c.1900 (Little Mount,
Kentucky, 1920 US census)

Pansy Daffodil Parcell
Born South Stoneham, Hampshire, 1902

Baptise Pumpkinseed
Born 2 March 1923; died Torrington,
Wyoming, USA, 4 May 2001

Seaflower Rolls

Born Cookham, Berkshire, 1875
*Seaflower was the sister of Benbow, Bluebell, Daisy,
May, Ocean and Snowdrop Rolls.*

Wood Sapp

(Male) Born Missouri c.1889
(Boone, Missouri, 1910 US census)

Mitchell Big Tree

Born Chorlton, Lancashire, 1896

Wigfall Weed

Born New York c.1862
(Jersey City, New Jersey, 1880 US census)

Primrose Wood

Born Hull, Yorkshire, c.1894
(Sculcoates, Yorkshire, 1901 England census)

Marvellous Monsters and Myths

Fairy Baker
Born 4 May 1897; died Springboro,
Ohio, USA, 8 December 1983

Ogre Bee
(Female) Born Ireland *c.*1883
(Manhattan, New York, 1910 US census)

Gnome Burgess
Born 29 May 1906; died Fort Wayne,
Indiana, USA, 30 July 1995

Giant Butler
Born 7 August 1908; died Palm Beach,
Florida, USA, 3 June 2002

Ogre Crumpler
(Female) Born Virginia *c.*1916
(Jerusalem, Virginia, 1920 US census)

George Dragon
Born *c.*1698; baptized St Katherine Creechurch,
London, 10 February 1704

Wolf Elf
Born St George in the East, London, 1901

Britain Ghost

Married John Gillett, Great Berkhampstead,
Hertfordshire, 14 October 1777

George Goblin

Married Maria Boot, Whorlton, Yorkshire, 11 June 1805

Minnie Gremlin

Born New York 1898 (Brooklyn, New York, 1900 US census)

Chimera Griffin

(Female) Born North Carolina c.1863
(Henderson, North Carolina, 1880 US census)
*Her name combines two imaginary creatures; according to
legend, the chimera had the head of a goat, the body of a
lioness and a tail ending in a snake's head, while the griffin
had a lion's body and the head and wings of an eagle.*

Horrid Griffin

(Male) Born Mississippi c.1878
(Adams, Mississippi, 1880 US census)

Ghoul Hall

(Male) Born Kentucky c.1891 (Saline, Ohio, 1930 US census)

Ghoul Hopkins Sr

Born 18 April 1891; died Stockton,
California, USA, January 1983
*His son, Ghoul Hopkins Jr, was born on 14 November 1932
and died in Las Vegas, Nevada, 1 March 1999.*

Fairy Laughter

Born 4 January 1907; died Campobello,
South Carolina, USA, September 1978

Fairy Lightfoot
Baptized Turvey, Bedfordshire, 3 March 1748
Fairy was the son of Richard and Elizabeth Lightfoot. When he grew up, he married someone called Mary, so they would have been known as Fairy and Mary. They had a son who they also called Fairy, who was baptized in Turvey on 2 September 1781 and died on 15 December 1784.

Minnie Monster
Born Colorado c.1849 (Keokuk, Iowa, 1885 Iowa, USA, census)

Minnie Ogre
Born Ireland c.1861 (Sioux Falls, Dakota Territory, 1880 US census)

William Sawyer Pixie
Baptized Horsham, Sussex, 2 November 1860

Goblin Reeves
Born Orsett, Essex, 1848

Phantom Simpson
(Male) Born Tennessee *c*.1838
(Gibson, Tennessee, 1850 US census)

Emma Troll
Born Marylebone, London, 1845

Phoenix Claw Unicorn
Born Darlington, Durham, 2002
Anther name that combines two mythological creatures:
the phoenix is a bird that is burned but then re-born out
of the flames, and a unicorn is a magical horse-like
animal with a single horn.

Otto Vampire
Born Oregon *c*.1851 (Cheyenne, Wyoming, 1880 US census)

Frances Ware Wolf
Born Lancaster, South Carolina, 5 October 1888;
died Pineville, North Carolina, USA, 21 March 1964

Anna Zombie
Born Poland *c*.1860 (Warren, Rhode Island, 1930 US census)
Now a feature of horror films such as Shaun of the Dead,
zombies, 'undead' humans, were first mentioned with
this spelling ('zombi' had been used earlier)
in 1929 in a book called Magic Island.

Guillaume Zombie
Baptized Vincennes, Indiana, USA, 3 February 1839;
married Livia Sweatland, Vincennes, 4 January 1869

Bizarre Bodies, Dotty Diseases and Dead Ends

BIZARRE BODIES

Legs Aftergut
Born California c.1900 (West Bear River, California, 1920 US census)

Adams Apple
Born Ohio 1938 (Johnson, Ohio, 1900 US census)

Amelia Backside
Born c.1926 (Wayne, Michigan, 1930 US census)

Lizzy Barelegs
Born Hitchin, Hertfordshire, 1872

Rosalind Silver Beard
Born Edmonton, Middlesex, 1883

Tonsil Beard
Born Arkansas c.1872 (Cache, Arkansas, 1930 US census)

Wealthy Beard
Married Gloucester, 1867

Hugh Belly
Born Ireland c.1801 (Liverpool,
Lancashire, 1851 England census)

Charles Bigfoot
Married Eleanor Cummin, Aycliffe, Durham,
15 November 1767

Bridget Blackeye
Married Richard Jones, London, 1 May 1617

Benjamin Blister
Married Wantage, Berkshire, 1847

Annie Body
Born Plympton St Mary, Devon, 1866

Trinkle Bott
Born Bristol, Tennessee, USA, 27 October 1921

Artie Bottom
Born Alabama c.1909 (Dundee, Alabama, 1910 US census)

Eunice Bottom
Married Henry Badger, Peru,
Massachusetts, America, 18 September 1787

Original Bottom
Born Lockwood, Yorkshire, 1846

Pleasant Bottom
(Male) Born Kentucky c.1832 (Baton Rouge,
Kentucky, 1880 US census)

Silence Bottom
Married Thomas Mason, Chesterfield,
Derbyshire, 26 October 1735

Huga Bottome
Baptized St Margaret's, Leicester, 10 March 1615

James Seymour Bottoms
Born Ampthill, Bedfordshire, 1898

Pinky Bottoms
Born Missouri 1887 (Pacific City, Missouri, 1900 US census)

Caesar Bowlegs
Born Oklahoma c.1840 (Brown, Oklahoma, 1910 US census)

Harry Liver Brain
Born Wortley, Yorkshire, 1877

I. Brow
Baptized Old Machar, Aberdeen, 20 August 1724

Georgius Bum
Born Litobratrice, Czechoslovakia, 31 March 1735

Minnie Bum
Born Toronto, Ontario, Canada, December 1874
(Ottawa City, Ontario, 1911 census of Canada)

Violet Bum
Born Birmingham, Warwickshire, c.1897
(Aston, Warwickshire, 1901 England census)

Herbush Bumbum
(Male) Born c.1859 (Ashby, Massachusetts, 1860 US census)

Iva Bump
Born Wisconsin 1867 (Macon, Illinois, 1900 US census)

Hugh Bums
Born Glasgow, Lanarkshire, *c*.1897
(Glasgow, 1901 Scotland census)

Belle Button
Born Salehurst, Sussex, *c*.1873
(Salehurst, 1891 England census)

Scary Butts
(Male) Born Kentucky *c*.1888 (Simpson,
Kentucky, 1910 US census)

Seymour Butts
Born New York *c*.1807 (Windsor, New York, 1850 US census)

Rosie Cheek
Born Hoddesdon, Hertfordshire, *c*.1905
(Hoddesdon, 1911 England census)

Christopher Ears
Of Kenwyn, Cornwall (will, 1790)

Knee Edge
(Male) Born England *c*.1802; died Kings,
New York, USA, August 1849

Rochmar Elbow
Married John Lyon, St Martin-in-the-Fields,
London, 29 May 1809

Odessa Eyeball
Born Indiana *c*.1882 (Marion, Indiana, 1920 US census)

Funny Face
(Female) Born Wyoming *c*.1879 (Fremont,
Wyoming, 1900 US census)

Gobo Fangs
Born Africa *c*.1850 (Grantsville City, Utah, 1880 US census)

Bird Fingernail
Born 12 June 1900; died Hammon,
Oklahoma, USA, July 1975

Brane B. Fingeroff
(Female) Born *c*.1881; passenger on *Chemnitz*, Bremen,
Germany–Baltimore, Maryland, USA, arrived 17 July 1904

Fred Fingers
Born 4 May 1907; died Frederickstown,
Missouri, USA, August 1979

Rosina Knee Flower
Born Henley, Buckinghamshire, 1868

James Hoot Foot
Born Shaftesbury, Dorset, 1843

Phoebe Forehead
Baptized Shanklin, Isle of Wight, 6 April 1788

John Tummy Hague
Born Ecclesall Bierlow, Yorkshire, 1910

Hairy Head
Born Dover, Kent, *c*.1878 (Dover, 1891 England census)

Heron Her Head
Born *c*.1901; died Arkansas, USA, April 1945

Orange Head
Born North Huish, Devon, *c*.1785
(Ugborough, Devon, 1861 England census)

Peaceful Heart
Born 17 December 1895; died Philadelphia,
Pennsylvania, USA, March 1967

Esther Elizabeth Highbottom
Born St Martin-in-the-Fields, London, 1846

Ambrose Hughbottom
Born England c.1830 (Edinburgh, 1861 Scotland census)

Body Hunter
(Female) Married Daniel Nippers, Lincoln,
Tennessee, USA, 24 June 1882

Blanche Kidney
Born Brentford, Middlesex, 1898

I. Lash
(Male) Born Poplar, London, c.1890
(Wanstead, Essex, 1901 England census)

Jemima Foot Legg
Born Dorchester, Dorset, 1841

Soppy Leggs
(Female) Born Bethnal Green, London
(Bethnal Green, 1901 England census)

I. Lid
Born Tomrefjord, Norway, 18 July 1847

Ruby Lips
Born Missouri c.1900 (Marie, North Dakota, 1910 US census)

Iva Longbottom
Born Balby, Yorkshire, c.1899
(Selby, Yorkshire, 1901 England census)

Lightfoot Longbottom
(Male) Born North Bierley, Yorkshire, 1900

Emma Longleg
Married Islington, London, 1911

Catherine Longlegs
Born Hesse-Darmstadt, Germany, c.1855
(Brooklyn, Illinois, 1870 US census)

James Lowbottom
Born Liverpool, Lancashire, c.1829
(Wardleworth, Lancashire, 1851 England census)

Hairy Mann
Married Dover, Kent, 1894

Willy McBum
Born Glasgow, Lanarkshire, c.1870
(Litherland, Lancashire, 1891 England census)

Willie McKnuckles
Born Arkansas c.1898 (Chicago, Illinois, 1930 US census)

Amelia Mouth
Born Stepney, London, 1842

Isabella Mybum
Born Guernsey, Channel Islands, c.1834
(Ilminster, Somerset, 1851 England census)

Toe Nail
(Female) Born c.1830 (South Dakota, 1897 US Indian census)

Fathalla Naked
Born 15 July 1886; died Toledo, Ohio, USA, August 1966

Old Man Neck
Born California *c.*1810 (Humboldt,
California, 1880 US census)

Naomi Nerve
Born Iden, Sussex, *c.*1824
(Playden, Kent, 1851 England census)

Knee Nickings
(Male) Born Virginia *c.*1843
(Marshall, Virginia, 1920 US census)

Madge Red Nose
Born Montana *c.*1916 (Big Horn, Montana, 1930 US census)

Nellie Nose
Baptized St Mary Redcliffe, Bristol,
Gloucestershire, 31 May 1877

Annie Nude
Born Stevenage, Hertfordshire, *c.*1866
(Stevenage, 1911 England census)

Lydia Pelvis
Baptized Bearstead, Kent, 24 January 1808

Gene Pool
Born Kentucky *c.*1876 (Caneyville, Kentucky, 1930 US census)

William Pulse
Died West Derby, Lancashire, 1880

Tonsil Queen
(Female) Born Georgia *c.*1875 (Bryant,
Georgia, 1910 US census)

Wonderful Ramsbottom
Born Dewsbury, Yorkshire, 1855

Nanny Rawbottom
Baptized Aston, Yorkshire, 5 April 1795

Jane Rockbottom
Born Birmingham, Warwickshire, c.1811
(Birmingham, 1841 England census)

Minnie Rosebottom
Born Ashton-under-Lyne, Lancashire, c.1888
(Ashton-under-Lyne, 1901 England census)

Mary Roughbottom
Baptized St Mary's, Oldham, Lancashire, 17 January 1731

Lincoln Entwistle Shipperbottom
Born Bolton, Lancashire, 1894

Obadiah Shoebottom
Baptized Rushton Spencer, Staffordshire, 26 March 1769

Winderlyn Shoulderblade
Born 16 February 1951; died Lame Deer,
Montana, USA, 4 November 2004

Benigna Shufflebottom
Died Haslingden, Lancashire, 1867

Hannah Skeleton
Born Great Boughton, Cheshire, 1867

Artery Smith
(Male) Born Bedstone, Shropshire, c.1899
(Bishops Castle, Shropshire, 1901 England census)

Fang Smith
(Female) Born Hopesay, Shropshire, c.1848
(Woolston, Shropshire, 1851 England census)

Joannes Mauritius Spleen
Baptized Gosport, Hampshire, 24 June 1789

Alice Nude Stibbs
Born c.1873 (East Hendred, Berkshire, 1911 England census)

Caroline Stomach
Born Rotherham, Yorkshire, 1878

Sarah Thickbottom
Died Wakefield, Yorkshire, 1879

Tobias Thumb
Baptized Greystoke, Cumberland, 16 August 1690

Charity Tiptoe
Married John Grundy, Westminster, London, 6 November 1730

Truelove Toe
Born Barrow upon Soar, Leicestershire, 1848

Mary Six Toes
Married Claude Eagle Pipe, Mellette,
South Dakota, USA, 12 November 1927

Bold Tongue
Married Bury, Lancashire, 1846

Pearl Tooth
Born 31 December 1907; died Maywood,
Illinois, USA, 27 September 1984

Sniffy Tubbs
(Female) Born Texas c.1878
(Montgomery, Texas, 1880 US census)

Ada Whisker Whisker
Born Walsingham, Norfolk, 1876

Ole O. Wig
Born Norway c.1801 (Lund, Minnesota, 1880 US census)
*Ole O. Wig had a son with exactly the
same name, born in 1829.*

Robert Valiant Wigg
Born London c.1875 (Hackney, London, 1881 England census)

Shakespeare Winterbottom
Married, Aston, Warwickshire, 1847

Naked Woman
Born c.1837 (Cheyenne, Montana, 1889 US Indian census)

John Woodenlegs
Born 12 November 1909; died Yellowstone,
Montana, USA, 17 December 1981

Ah Yawn
Born China c.1841 (Modesto, California, 1880 US census)

DOTTY DISEASES
• • • • • • • • • • • • • •

Elizabeth Agony
Married Wrexham, Denbighshire, 1849

Filadofo Aspirin
Born 30 March 1914; died Lake Forest,
California, USA, 30 May 1998

Sarah Bandage
Married John Chase, St Martin-in-the-Fields,
London, 20 May 1823

Minnie Bruiser
Born Illinois c.1863 (Chicago, Illinois, 1910 US census)

Hygiene Bybee
(Female) Born Iowa c.1909 (Washington,
Iowa, 1910 US census)

Ah Choo
Married Stepney, London, 1882

Felix Plague Delarombe
Married Christchurch, Hampshire, 1874

Dan Druff
Born Kentucky c.1841 (Perry, Kentucky, 1850 US census)

Harriet Thrower Fitts
Born Granville, North Carolina, USA, 9 January 1893

Frances Flu
Married Anne Richardson, Westminster,
London, 18 March 1724

Acne Fountain
Born North Carolina c.1871 (Richlands,
North Carolina, 1930 US census)

Lazarus Getsick
Born Stoke-on-Trent, Staffordshire, 1905

Salmon Headache
Born South Dakota c.1845
(South Rouse, South Dakota, 1910 US census)

Richard Hiccup
Baptized Twyning, Gloucestershire, 24 March 1782

Henry Hiccups
Born Westbury-on-Severn, Gloucestershire, 1852

Plague Hopp
Born Wisconsin c.1885 (Westford,
Wisconsin, 1910 US census)

Eczema Hugey
(Female) Born Ohio 1878 (Burlington Junction,
Missouri, 1900 US census)

Estelle Hurts
Born Sandal Magna, Yorkshire, c.1886
(Sandal Magna, 1891 England census)

Giggi Regina Ichinose
Born 22 June 1942; died Chino Valley,
Arizona, USA, 9 October 2008

Isabella Itch
Married John Heyworth, Newchurch-in-Rossendale,
Lancashire, 8 June 1875

Tonsilliti Jackson
Born 7 November 1932; died Long Beach,
California, USA, 26 May 2006

Surgeon Kershaw
Born Basford, Nottinghamshire, 1860
'Surgeon' was his first name.

Merrie Leper
Born c.1801 (Glasgow, 1841 Scotland census)

Martha Lergy
Married Ormskirk, Lancashire, 1865

Samuel Measles
Baptized Welford-on-Avon, Gloucestershire, 8 April 1747

Richard Mumps
Born Salford, Lancashire, 1864

Aspirin Olsen
Born Norway c.1856 (Traill, Dakota Territory, 1880 US census)

Coard Squarey Pain
Born Wandsworth, London, 1851

Constant Pain
(Female) Born Hackney, London, 1901
(Hackney, 1901 England census)

Edward Steady Pain
Born Dover, Kent, 1891

Ima Pain
Born Georgia 1891 (Clark, Georgia, 1900 US census)

Iva Pain
Born Missouri *c.*1896 (Elsmore, Kansas, 1910 US census)

Benjamin Sharpe Paine
Born *c.*1845; died Brentford, Middlesex, 1875

Instance Ann Pill
Born Cardiff, Glamorgan, 1871

Mary Pimple
Born Bridport, Dorset, 1852

Emily Frances Plague
Married Stroud, Gloucestershire, 1865

Lovina Plague
Born Michigan 1850 (Van Buren, Michigan, 1880 US census)

Iva Rash
Born Kansas, USA, 23 May 1902; died San Bernardino,
California, USA, 10 June 1981

Ann Sneezy
Married Robert Clark Tetford, St Giles without Cripplegate,
London, December 1974

Malaria Strunk
Born Pennsylvania c.1875 (Brecknock,
Pennsylvania, 1880 US census)

Hugh Swelling
Born Ireland c.1811 (Kilbirnie, Ayrshire, 1851 Scotland census)

Smallpox Tommy
Born Florida c.1887 (Lee, Florida, 1930 US census)

Ella D. Toothache
Married Theodor C. Teeple, Ken, Michigan,
USA, 22 September 1908

Prudence Toothaker
Married William Avery, St Olave's, Southwark,
London, 26 January 1789

Phobia Wass
(Female) Born Calland, Derbyshire, c.1865
(Standish, Lancashire, 1891 England census)

Betsey Wrinkle
Married Bolton, Lancashire, 1837

DEAD ENDS
• • • • • • • • •

Mary Carcass
Born Reading, Berkshire, c.1863
(Horsham, Sussex, 1881 England census)
*Mary Carcass gave her profession in the census as
'Punch and Judy performer'.*

James Cemetery
Died Liverpool, Lancashire, 1844

Elmyra S. Small Coffin

(Female) Born Maine c.1895 (Mechanic Falls,
Maine, 1920 US census)

Samuel Lowery Coffin Coffin

Born Hoo, Kent, 1843

Violet Corpse

Born Whitby, Yorkshire, 1891

Helen A. Deadbody

Born Northamptonshire c.1875 (St John, Cheshire,
1881 England census)

Archibald Deadly

Born Paddington, London, c.1875 (St Gregory by Paul's,
London, 1891 England census)

Grimwood Death

Born c.1810; died Hartismere, Suffolk, 1884
*Several generations of boys in the family were
given the name Grimwood Death.*

Lazarus Death

Born Cambridge 1844

Thomas Jolly Death

Born City of London c.1843; died Epsom, Surrey, 1908

Dominick Doom

Born Somerset c.1845 (Whitchurch,
Herefordshire, 1861 England census)

Phil Graves

Died Rotherham, Yorkshire, 1879

Toilet Titters

Urine Adkins
Born 15 June 1896; died Coeburn, Virginia, USA, March, 1972

Farty Archibald
(Female) Born USA 15 November 1876 (New Westminster,
British Columbia, 1901 Canada census)

Boadicea Belch
Baptized Rickmansworth, Hertfordshire, 2 May 1808

Costly Belcher
(Male) Born Virginia c.1845 (Smiths River, Virginia,
1880 US census)

Bogey Boe
(Female) Born c.1812; passenger on *Emily*, Liverpool,
UK–New York, USA, arrived 2 August 1932

Urina Buckett
Born Isle of Wight 1867

Judge Burpo
Born 17 June 1923 (Marengo, Alabama, 1930 US census)

Richard Burpy
Born 5 May 1816; Baptized Wesleyan Methodist,
Frome, Somerset, 26 October 1817

Farting Clack
Born London, *c.*1863 (Walthamstow, Essex,
1871 England census)

Farter Craven
Born Thornton, Yorkshire, *c.*1833
(Bradford, Yorkshire, 1871 England census)

Magnolia Fart
Born *c.*1930 (Jackson, Madison, Tennessee, 1930 US census)

Minnie Fart
Born Martock, Somerset, *c.*1875 (Ravenstone with Snibston,
Leicestershire, 1901 England census)

Street Fart
(Male) Born Arkansas *c.*1868
(McConnell, Arkansas, 1880 US census)

Urine Fartabella
Born Italy *c.*1896 (East Youngstown, Ohio, 1920 US census)

Betsey Farting
Born Samford, Suffolk, 1843

Fritz Farting
Born Prussia c.1858; passenger on *Silesia*, Hamburg,
Germany–New York, USA, arrived 20 November 1883

Gertrud Farts
Married Diedrich Bergkamper, Soest, Prussia, 7 October 1819

Ramona Farts
Born Vivero, Spain, c.1874 (New Brighton,
Cheshire, 1911 England census)

Zama N. Fartwell
Born Vermont c.1830 (Albany, Vermont, 1880 US census)

Bridget Farty
Married John Connoly, Greenock,
Renfrewshire, 17 October 1864

Nappy Farty
Married Tynemouth, Northumberland, 1853

Marie Fartz
Born Kansas c.1887 (Horse Creek, Wyoming, 1920 US census)

Gladys Toilet Fenton
Born Monmouth c.1890 (Shirehampton,
Gloucestershire, 1891 England census)

Farty Gladwish
Born Hastings, Sussex, c.1882 (Hastings, 1901 England census)

Mary Gofarty
Born Ireland c.1857 (Liverpool, Lancashire,
1881 England census)

Burpy Loomer
Born Brighton, Massachusetts, USA, 16 June 1869

Puke Looper
Born Oklahoma c.1918 (Lewis, Oklahoma, 1920 US census)

Leo La Pee
Born 30 July 1906; died Sullivan Missouri, USA, July 1987

Loo Loo
Born c.1877; died Greenwich, London, 1904

Patrick McFart
Born Ireland c.1828 (New Monkland,
Lanarkshire, 1851 Scotland census)

Willy McPee
Born Wigtown, Dumfries, c.1781
(Hackney, London, 1861 England census)

Agnes McWee
Born Dundee, Forfarshire, c.1877
(Solihull, Warwickshire, 1911 England census)

Lou Paper
(Female) Born Watford, Hertfordshire, c.1858
(Lambeth, London, 1891 England census)

Ada Pee
Born Manchester c.1892 (Manchester, 1911 England census)

Alice May Pee
Born Cheslyn Hay, Staffordshire, c.1902
(Cheslyn Hay, 1911 England census)

Blondine Pee
Married Richard Bryant, Clark, Texas, USA, 5 August 1976

Florence May Pee
Born Aston, Warwickshire, 1895

Hannah Pees
Married John Walker, Whorlton, Yorkshire, 16 May 1808

Ada Poo
Born Poplar, London, c.1889 (Poplar, 1911 England census)

Ah Poo
Born Hong Kong c.1866
(Stepney, London, 1911 England census)

Angel Poo
Born Spain c.1886; crew on *Cristóbal Colón*, Bilbao,
Spain–New York, USA, arrived 21 June 1929

Ellis Poo Poo
Born Leeds, Yorkshire, 1842

Lotta Poo
(Male) Married Hana Kalenahi, Hawaii, 15 February 1871

Pedro Poo
Born Comillas, Spain, 24 January 1809

Burpy Prouty
Baptized Lancaster, Massachusetts, USA, 18 March 1764

Charity Puke
Married George Addison, St Mary's, Kingston upon Hull,
Yorkshire, 15 October 1802

Toilet Queen
(Female) Born Iowa 1890 (Ashton, Iowa, 1900 US census)

Farty Ray
Born Tennessee *c*.1813 (Clarksville, Texas, 1860 US census)

Lou Roll
Born Uxbridge, Middlesex, 1902

Ida Seafart
Born Pennsylvania *c*.1879 (Niles, Ohio, 1880 US census)

Max Seafart
Born North Dakota *c*.1907
(Souris, North Dakota, 1920 US census)

Robert Potty Seward
Born Ulverston, Cumbria, 1882

Sarah Sick
Baptized Saxby, Leicestershire, 26 May 1811

Ulalia Tinkle
Married Henry Stephens, Littleham by
Bideford, Devon, 29 December 1699

Zenobia Urine
Baptized Wendron, Cornwall, 24 May 1799

Ah Wee We
Born *c*.1869; died Hartlepool, Durham, 1909

Hugh Wee
Married Rachel Higgenbottom, St Mary,
Radcliffe, Lancashire, 8 July 1832

Jasmine May Wee
Born Bristol 1991

Christian Weegood

(Female) Married Arthur Wills, St Edmund,
Salisbury, Wiltshire, 14 January 1625

Maria Weewee

Born New York, USA, 12 May 1855

W. C. Weewie

Born c.1904; died Everett, Washington, USA, 2 February 1981

Mabel Widdle

Born Ferriby, Lincolnshire, c.1890
(Thorne, Yorkshire, 1911 England census)

James Windbottom

Born Salford, Lancashire, c.1853
(Salford, 1881 England census)

Fart Woman

Born c.1836 (South Dakota, 1891 US Indian census)

Freaky Food and Daft Drinks

Biscuit Adams
(Male) Born Georgia *c.*1800 (Beech Creek, Arkansas, 1850 US census)

Catherine Pizza Alexander
Married Plomesgate, Suffolk, 1847

Blanche Almond
Born Crawshawbooth, Lancashire, *c.*1890 (Crawshawbooth, 1891 England census)

Cheerful Hyacinth Apple
Born Illinois 1896 (El Centro, California, 1920 US census)

Paul Artichoke
Born Russia 24 May 1894 (Syracuse, New York, USA, First World War draft registration)

London Asparagus
Born Pennsylvania 1849 (Charlestown, Pennsylvania, 1900 US census)

Tom Ato
Born Sleaford, Lincolnshire, 1867

Bum B. Bacon
Married Kenosha, Wisconsin, USA, 12 September 1900

Chris P. Bacon
Born 7 April 1920; died South Burlington,
Vermont, USA, 30 January 1997

Delicious Bacon
(Female) Born Georgia 1895 (Reidsville Town,
Georgia, 1900 US census)

Eggy Bacon
Born Georgia c.1851 (Hawkinsville, Georgia, 1880 US census)

Hairy Bacon
Born Delaware 1900 (Laurel, Delaware, 1900 US census)

Jane Fat Bacon
Born Rippingale, Lincolnshire, c.1811
(Rippingale, 1851 England census)

Lean Bacon
Born Pennsylvania c.1876 (Tioga,
Pennsylvania, 1910 US census)

Liver Bacon
(Male) Born Missouri c.1891 (St Charles,
Missouri, 1910 US census)

Lucious [*sic*] Bacon
Born 2 August 1906; died Savannah,
Georgia, USA, September 1977

Silence Bacon
(Female) Born South Normanton, Derbyshire, c.1822
(South Normanton, 1871 England census)

Roy Baguette
Born 1945; died Cheshire, 2004

Catherine Banana
Born Barnsley, Yorkshire, 1876

Etta Banana
Born 17 June 1920; died Miami, Florida, USA, 9 May 1994

Edward Mars Barr
Born 15 August 1899 (Hancock, West Virginia, USA, First World War draft registration)

Henrietta Bean
Married Henry Haveman, St Matthew's, Bethnal Green, London, 19 September 1768

Mary Little Bean
Born Alabama c.1853 (Phillips, Alabama, 1910 US census)

Rhubarb Bean
Born 1916; died Bury St Edmunds, Suffolk, 2002

Snickers Beaty
Born England c.1862 (Humboldt, Iowa, USA, 1895 Iowa census)

Hungry Bill
Born Nevada c.1851 (Eureka, Nevada, 1880 US census)

John William Biscuit
Born Oldham, Lancashire, 1870

Nora Bone
Born South Stoneham, Hampshire, 1902

Jedidah A. Breakfast
Married Richard A. Newberry, Exeter, Devon, 1999

Pepsi Cola Brown
Born 25 May 1908; died Bridgeport, Fairfield,
Connecticut, USA, December 1987

Lunch Buffaloe
Born North Carolina, USA, 12 April 1912; died
Roanoke Rapids, North Carolina, 31 December 1969

Maud Stale Bun
Born Sunderland, Durham, c.1851
(Sunderland, 1871 England census)

Dieter Burger
Born Illinois c.1904 (Madison, Illinois, 1920 US census)

Ham Burger
Born Michigan c.1847 (Pittsford, Michigan, 1850 US census)

Roland Butter
Born Pennsylvania c.1862
(Boggs, Pennsylvania, 1870 US census)

Royal Butter
Born USA 6 April 1889 (Sherbrooke,
Quebec, 1901 Canada census)

Etta Cabbage
Born McLean, Kentucky, USA, 23 April 1931

Henrietta Cake
Born 12 May 1820; baptized St Edmund,
Salisbury, Wiltshire, 29 May 1820

Flossie Candy
Born Shepton Mallet, Somerset, c.1858
(Wincanton, Somerset, 1871 England census)

Hattie Cauliflower
Married James Busby, McDonough,
Illinois, USA, 17 January 1879

Lemon Cauliflower
Born Pennsylvania c.1871 (Blair,
Pennsylvania, 1910 US census)

Henrietta Celery
Born Louisiana 1890 (New Orleans,
Louisiana, 1900 US census)

Charles Cheese
Baptized St Peter and St Paul, Milton-next-Gravesend,
Kent, 22 February 1700

Louise Cheese
Born New York 1909 (Altamont, New York, 1910 US census)

Marmalade Tangerine Cherbert
Born 22 March 1944; died Coos Bay,
Oregon, USA, 4 April 2004

Etta Cherry
Born 28 April 1898; died Jamaica,
New York, USA, August 1977

Monster Cherry
(Male) Born Florida c.1904 (Bland, Florida, 1910 US census)

Etta Chicken
Born Russia c.1883 (Chicago, Illinois, 1910 US census)

Charles Chip
Baptized St Dunstan's, Stepney, London, 9 October 1808

Sarah Chocolate
Baptized Cranley, Surrey, 14 October 1693

Lydia Chutney
Born Illinois c.1861 (Okawville, Illinois, 1880 US census)

Sweetmeat Coach
Born 26 August 1895; died Chicago, Illinois, USA, April 1966

Cornelius Coffee
Baptized Phillack, Cornwall, 16 November 1868

William Honey Combs
Born St Cleer, Cornwall, c.1849
(St Cleer, 1891 England census)

Fortune Cook
(Female) Born Pennsylvania c.1805 (Marieta,
Ohio, 1880 US census)

Gravy Cook
Born 18 December 1917; died Mississippi, USA, May 1961

Humiliation Cook
Died Ipswich, Suffolk, 1848

Sardine Cook
(Male) Born Kentucky c.1863
(Tracy, Kentucky, 1880 US census)

Walter Cress
Married Sarah Wilton, St Mary the Virgin, Dover,
Kent, 21 May 1805

Christiana Crisps
Married William Woodward, Goldington,
Bedfordshire, 22 October 1571

Millie Cucumber
Born Whitechapel, London, 1885

Claude De Grouchy Curry
Born Newport, Monmouthshire, 1897

Double Curry
(Male) Born Louisiana *c*.1907 (Ouachita,
Louisiana, 1910 US census)

Custard Custard
Born *c*.1876 (Tanners Creek, Virginia, 1930 US census)

Lemonade Danforth
(Male) Born Kansas *c*.1879 (Burlingame,
Kansas, 1880 US census)

Toast Deadman
Born Texas *c*.1882 (Lamar, Texas, 1910 US census)

Etta De Cow
Born Des Moines, Iowa, *c*.1883 (Des Moines, 1925
Iowa state census)

Louisa F. De la Sausage
Born Kentish Town, London, *c*.1844 (Enfield,
Middlesex, 1871 England census)

Marie Etta Dinner
Born New York 1899 (Montclair, New Jersey, 1900 US census)

Onlla Jane Doughnut
Married Henry J. Secrist, Richland, Ohio, USA, 19 July 1863

Anice Drybread
Born Nineveh Township, Indiana, USA, 30 March 1883

Chris P. Duck
Born Amersham, Buckinghamshire, 1964

Etta Duck
Born 4 December 1921; died Suffolk,
Virginia, USA, 12 December 1999

Marmalade Duke
(Male) Born England c.1815 (De Kalb,Illinois, 1880 US census)

Treacle Ebersole
Born Texas, USA, 19 February 1902; died San Diego,
California, 30 August 1993

Frida Egg
Born 28 April 1861; married Albert Ernst, Thurgau,
Switzerland, 28 October 1890

Richard Bacon Eggar
Born Alton, Hampshire, 1861

Paprika Fahrenwald
Born San Francisco, California, USA, 11 August 1972
Her sister Ginger was born in San Francisco on 1 July 1974.

Fat Meat Fields
(Female) Born Mississippi 1897 (Holmes,
Mississippi, 1900 US census)

Fishel Finger
Born Austria c.1861 (Brooklyn, New York, 1930 US census)

Chipman Fish
Married Betsey Howland, Sandwich,
Massachusetts, USA, 11 February 1792

Philetus Fish
(Male) Born Uxbridge, Middlesex, 1844

Tuna Fish
Born Iowa c.1886 (Topeka, Kansas, 1930 US census)

Colly Flower
Father of Rebecca Flower, born 7 September 1797; baptized
St Anne's, Soho, London, 24 September 1797

Scooter J. Foody
Born Nottingham 1996

Amber Fudge
Born Salisbury, Wiltshire, 2000

Spicy Fudge
(Female) Born Georgia c.1859 (Pinellas, 1935
Florida, USA, census)

Eliza Sandwich Fuller
Born c.1861 (Willesden, London, 1911 England census)

Frank Furter
Born 3 August 1889; died Russellton,
Pennsylvania, USA, June 1972

Prudence Pineapple Goodall
Born Stoke-on-Trent, Staffordshire, 1989
*She is believed to be the only British
baby to be named Pineapple.*

Rosetta Gooseberry
Born 9 October 1921; died New Orleans,
Louisiana, USA, 6 August 2004

Mountain Gravy
Baptized North Walsham, Norfolk, 15 May 1774

Lettuce Green
Born Hyde, North Carolina, USA, 2 September 1912

Lovonie Grub
Married Arthur Gost, Union,
Tennessee, USA, 3 September 1899

Lotta Ham
Born Massachusetts c.1877 (Somerville,
Massachusetts, 1880 US census)

Petronella Hamburger
Born Islington, London, 1876

Spearmint Hardy
Born Blandford, Dorset, 1906

Crystal Lollipop Hernandez
Born Sacramento, California, USA, 6 May 1980

Butter Hubbard
Born 27 February 1907; died Birmingham,
Alabama, USA, August 1972

James Jam
Buried Camborne, Cornwall, 9 August 1772

Heather Jelly
Born Frome, Somerset, 1950

Watercress Joe
Born c.1829 (Burslem, Staffordshire, 1881 England census)
*'Watercress Joe' may have been his nickname, but that is his
name as it appears in the 1881 census.*

Chocolate Ethel Jones
Born Cirencester, Gloucestershire, *c.*1894
(Cirencester, 1911 England census)

George Ketchup
Baptized All Saints, Sudbury, Suffolk, 24 January 1803

Trifle Lafountan
(Male) Born Canada *c.*1852 (Bakersfield,
Vermont, 1870 US census)

Certain Lard
Born Louisiana *c.*1905 (Liberty Hill,
Louisiana, 1920 US census)

Daisy Lasagna
Born 1907; died Wandsworth, London, 1988

Turkey Legs
(Male) Born *c.*1865 (Oklahoma, 1895 US Indian census)

Orange V. Lemon
(Male) Born Indiana c.1846 (Marion, Indiana, 1850 US census)

Luscious Lemons
Born 24 July 1903; died Chickasha,
Oklahoma, USA, July 1969

Louisa Loaf
Born Middlesbrough, Yorkshire, 1897

Etta Lott
Born Mississippi c.1877 (Lamar, Mississippi, 1920 US census)

Elizabeth Macaroni
Born London c.1810 (Weybridge, Surrey,
1881 England census)

Percy MacBurger
Born Pennsylvania c.1880 (Philadelphia,
Pennsylvania, 1910 US census)

Marcia Mallow
Born Michigan 1890 (Athens Village,
Michigan, 1900 US census)

Alfred Mash Mash
Born Mitford, Norfolk, 1851

Tomato May
Born St Saviour, Southwark, London, 1889

Orange Vanilla McClendon
Born Florida, USA, c.1934 (1945 Florida census)

Scarlett Marmalade McCormack
Born Plymouth, Devon, 2004

Walter Mellon
Born Salford, Lancashire, 1839

Kathleen Lovett Milkshake
Married Edward Dana Densmore,
Maine, USA, 26 March 1993

John Beard Mince
Born 8 December 1804; baptized St Leonard,
Shoreditch, London, 21 April 1819

Merriment Marmite
Chocolate Mistrano
Born Cambridge 2004

Pepper Mixer
Born Dedham, Massachusetts, USA;
changed his name to Charles Mixer, 13 June 1810

Matilda Mushroom
Married John Shanks, Skirlaugh, Yorkshire, 1848

Martha Mustard
Married John Lunn, St Giles, Cripplegate,
London, 28 October 1662

Mustard M. Mustard
(Female) Born Illinois c.1921 (Belleville,
Illinois, 1930 US census)
It is believed that her middle name was also Mustard.

Nicholas Noodle
Born Manhattan, New York, USA, 29 September 1887

Hazel Nutt
Born Holborn, London, 1894

P. Nutt

Born Macclesfield, Cheshire, 1859

More recently, Peter Nutt, a teacher in Scunthorpe,
Lincolnshire, became annoyed when his students repeatedly
called him P. Nutt, and changed his surname to Knuddsen.

Lydia Omelette

Born Oakdale, Massachusetts, USA, 28 September 1895

Thankful Onion

Born Rhode Island *c*.1790 (North Kingstown,
Rhode Island, 1870 US census)

Lemon Orange

Baptized Newcastle-under-Lyme, Staffordshire, 28 July 1723

Memory D. Orange

(Male) Born Iowa *c*.1881 (Pilot Rock,
Oregon, 1910 US census)

Frederick Cheese Painter

Born Lambeth, London, 1859

Oliver Pancake

Born 4 November 1895; died Grosse Pointe,
Michigan, USA, June 1975

Pansy Pancake

Died Lawrence, Ohio, USA, 1 November 1910

Lotta Parsley

Born Indiana *c*.1889 (Hamblen, Indiana, 1910 US census)

Patsy Pasta

Born Italy *c*.1872 (Vandergrift Heights,
Pennsylvania, 1910 US census)

Stephen Pastry
Married Gabriela Barrow, All Saints, Newcastle upon Tyne,
Northumberland, 14 August 1716

Henrietta Peach
Born Burton upon Trent, Staffordshire, 1875

Preserved Pears
Resident of Rehoboth, Massachusetts, USA (1800 US census)

Gordon Salter Pepper
Born Blything, Suffolk, 1876

Sergeant Pepper
Born 12 May 1907; died Gladwne,
Pennsylvania, USA, March 1982

Farce Pickle
Born 26 September 1923; died Independence,
Missouri, USA, 24 March 2005

Apple Pie
(Male) Born Virginia c.1830 (Shelby,
Tennessee, 1870 US census)

Henryetta Pie
Born South Carolina c.1856 (Goethe,
South Carolina, 1910 US census)

Arthur Pint
Born Portsmouth, Hampshire, c.1797 ('brewer', Portsea,
Hampshire, 1851 England census)

Margherita Pizza
Born Italy c.1849; passenger on *Neckar*,
Naples, Italy–New York, USA, arrived 2 June 1907

George Pork
Married Jane Wetlock, Cathedral Church of St Thomas
of Canterbury, Portsmouth, Hampshire, 30 July 1827

Theophilus Porridge
Baptized Gravesend, Kent, 22 September 1752

Katie Kate Ka-ke-tah Potato
Born Flint, Oklahoma, USA, c.1851

Florence Gooseberry Pratt
Born Whitechapel, London, 1868

Strawberry E. Presnell
Married St Olave, Southwark, London, 1888

Hephzibah Pudding
Married Newington, London, 1845

Hugh Pudding
Married Elizabeth Thorne, Minterne Magna,
Dorset, 17 August 1731

Cheree Pye
Born Blackpool, Lancashire, 1994

Catherine Shepherd Pye
Born 25 November 1902; died Colchester, Essex, 1984

Shepherd Pyes
Born North Dakota, USA, 15 September 1889 (Grand Forks,
North Dakota, First World War draft registration)

Leaning Radish
Born Scotter, Lincolnshire, 1841

Éclair Rapper
(Male) Born c.1924 (Duquesne,
Pennsylvania, 1930 US census)

Olive Raspberry
Baptized Leesfield, Lancashire, 3 October 1883

Pleasant Raspberry
(Female) Born Brightlingsea, Essex, 1804

Angelina Ravioli
Born 14 May 1907; died Hartford,
Connecticut, USA, May 1969

Lucas Saide
Born Manchester, Lancashire, 1989

Green Salad
(Male) Born Texas c.1854 (Navaro, Texas, 1880 US census)

Magnolia Salad
Born 22 March 1922; died Phoenixville,
Pennsylvania, USA, 31 January 2005

Kicki Salami
(Male) Born Turkey c.1866 (Brooklyn,
New York, 1910 US census)

Tina Salmon
Born 8 November 1905; died Uvale,
Texas, USA, 3 January 1984

Ham Sandwich
Born c.1910 (New Orleans, Louisiana, 1910 US census)

Earnestine Sausage
Born 11 December 1908; died Clovis,
California, USA, 4 April 2002

Ada Scone
Born Pembroke 1905

Clementine Semolina
Born Westminster, London, c.1900
(Leyton, Essex, 1901 England census)
*At the time of the 1901 census, Clementine and her
older brother Hillary Semolina, born c.1896, were
in the care of the St Agnes Orphanage.*

Toffee Shaker
Born 23 July 1891; died Cleveland, Ohio, USA, May 1972

Toast Baker Sizum
Born Germany c.1899; crew on *Leviathan*, Southampton,
UK–New York, USA, arrived 26 April 1926

Tomato Slick Slaughter
Married Wanda Joy Canfield, Reno,
Nevada, USA, 3 August 1974

Lizzie Muffin Smith
Born Burton upon Trent, Staffordshire, 1898

Mango Smith
(Male) Born Scotland c.1804 (Litchurch,
Derbyshire, 1871 England census)

Pickles Smith
Born Burnley, Lancashire, 1863

Ruby Lee Cupcake Smith
Born *c*.1914; died Black Mountain,
North Carolina, USA, 8 July 2006

Dick Bean Soup
Born California *c*.1844 (Sonoma, California, 1860 US census)

Luigi Spaghetti
Born Italy *c*.1887; passenger on *New York*,
Southampton, UK–New York, USA, arrived 7 September 1913

Min Spiess
Born Laverton, Gloucestershire, *c*.1876
(Snowshill, Gloucestershire, 1891 England census)

Obadiah Sprouts
Died Leyburn, Yorkshire, 1862

Candy Store
Married Mark Szafranski, Clark, Nevada, USA, 20 May 2000

Phil Stuffing
Baptized Wellingore, Lincolnshire, 6 February 1779

Christian Syrup
(Male) Born Germany 1846 (Wawarsing,
New York, 1900 US census)

Cherry Tart
Born Mississippi *c*.1859 (Yalobusha,
Mississippi, 1860 US census)

Treacle Tart
Baptized Durham 21 June 1746

T. Time
Married Anne Delloe, Furneaux Pelham,
Hertfordshire, 26 April 1618

Mawdlyn Treacle
Baptized St Benet Fink, London, 24 September 1557

Thomas Vegetable
Born Tetnall, Staffordshire, c.1825 (Birmingham,
Warwickshire, 1851 census)

Victory P. Vinegar
(Female) Born Tennessee c.1851 (St Louis,
Missouri, 1880 US census)

Henrietta Waffle
Born 7 February 1918; died Renton,
Washington, USA, 18 November 2006

Raspberry Washington
Born 30 November 1916; died Jackson,
Mississippi, USA, 1 December 1995

Cornelious Mushroom Whiteman
Born 25 March 1882 (Jefferson, Pennsylvania,
USA, First World War draft registration)

Charles Cranberry Winfield
Married Gloucester 1850

Home Humour

Bertie Basin
Born Holborn, London, c.1891
(Clerkenwell, London, 1901 England census)

Peg Basket
Born Tennessee c.1836 (Wilson, Tennessee, 1870 US census)

Fancy Baskett
Married Steyning, Sussex, 1880

Duvet Batesole
Born Ohio c.1968 (Toledo, Ohio, 1870 US census)

Anita Bath
Born Wisconsin c.1802 (Milwaukee,
Wisconsin, 1920 US census)

Steve Bedroom
Born Austria c.1864 (Chicago, Illinois, 1910 US census)

Ella Door Bell
Died Ramsey, Minnesota, USA, 16 January 1929

Lydia Bin
Born Massachusetts, USA, c.1770; died
Florida, Massachusetts, 1850

Spanner Bing
Born Northwood, Isle of Wight, *c.*1822 (Newchurch, Hampshire, 1851 England census)

Phil Bins
Born Ohio *c.*1848 (Clay, Ohio, 1850 US census)

Flora Board
Born Stoke Damerel, Devon, 1872

Friend Bottle
Born Linstead, Kent, *c.*1813; died St Olave, Southwark, London, 1891

Letta Box
(Female) Born Virginia *c.*1910 (Marion, Virginia, 1920 US census)

Always Brick
(Male) Born Minnesota c.1895 (Stearns, Minnesota, 1920 US census)

House Brick
Born Virginia c.1913 (Henry, Virginia, 1930 US census)

Rhoda Broom
Baptized St Matthew's, Walsall, Staffordshire, 7 September 1795

William Broomhandle
(Birth place and date unknown; New York, 1840 US census)

Ina Buckett
Born c.1913 (Massilon, Illinois, 1930 US census)

Nimrod Buckett
Born Portsmouth, Hampshire, 1820

Joseph Greenhouse Careless
Born Walsall, Staffordshire, 1874

Dish Carrington
(Male) Born Dukinfield, Cheshire, c.1892 (Nether Hoyland, Yorkshire, 1901 England census)

Booker Case
Born Kentucky 1 April 1916; died Henryetta, Oklahoma, USA, March 1993

Scissors C. S. R. Coker
Born Dartford, Kent, 1915

Radio Cruell
Born 10 March 1915; died Greenville, South Carolina, USA, March 1983

Barbie Cue
Born Scotland *c.*1819 (Philadelphia,
Pennsylvania, 1880 US census)

T. Cupp
(Female) Born Beaminster, Dorset, 1876

Annette Curtain
Married Mitchell Riley, Nottingham, 1985

Philip Doorknob Delacruz
Born Los Angeles, California, USA, 22 October 1983

Bill Ding
Baptized Easton-on-the-Hill,
Northamptonshire, 22 September 1661

George Doorbell
Born Vermont *c.*1896 (Springfield
Massachusetts, 1930 US census)

Crystal Glass
Born *c.*1929 (Kickapoo, Wisconsin, 1930 US census)

Birdie Greenhouse
Born 11 August 1907; died Brooklyn,
New York, USA, 12 November 1992

Rusty Hammer
Born Alexander, North Carolina, USA, 1982

Bea Hives
Born Lambeth, London, 1887

Welcome Holmes
Born Pennsylvania *c.*1840 (Erie,
Pennsylvania, 1920 US census)

Ima Hoover
Born 17 February 1908; died Irene, Texas, USA, 13 July 1988

Wardrobe Hudson
Born East Retford, Nottinghamshire, 1857

Pongo Irons
Born 18 February 1921; died Broxbourne,
Hertfordshire, April 1996

Fridge Jester
Born Texas 25 October 1892; died Falls Church,
Virginia, USA, June 1973

Lydia Kettle
Born Marylebone, London, 1839

Brilliant B. Kitchens
Born 3 September 1920; died Orlando,
Florida, USA, 22 July 1994

Dora Knob
Born Ohio 1891 (McLean, Ohio, 1900 US census)

Aurelia Lookinglass
Born 24 June 1919; died Apache,
Oklahoma, USA, March 1979

Carpet Magruder
Born Texas c.1901 (San Jacinto, Texas, 1920 US census)

Dora Mat
Born Austria c.1892 (Manhattan, New York, 1910 US census)

Hannah Mattress
Died Bishop Auckland, Durham, 1859

Cupboard Middlebrooks
Born Georgia c.1879 (Morgan, Georgia, 1880 US census)

Lorna Mower
Born Utah c.1906 (Fairview, Utah, 1910 US census)

Ivan Oven
Born 2 August 1924; passenger on *Queen Elizabeth*, New York,
USA–Southampton, UK, arrived 13 December 1956

Wal Paper
Born Greenwich, Kent, c.1864
(Greenwich, 1901 England census)

Iva Pillow
Born 2 June 1901; died Lake Elsinore,
California, USA, 24 September 1982

Rusty Pipes
Born 23 April 1975; died Missouri, USA, 26 May 1995

Dina Plate
Born Wisconsin c.1872 (Rantoul, Wisconsin, 1880 US census)

Utensil Pugh
Married Michael Ward, Randolph,
North Carolina, USA, 6 October 1889

Bell Ringer
Married Door, Wisconsin, 20 August 1885
Bell Ringer lived in the county of Door.

Shower Rose
(Male) Born Virginia c.1864 (Union,
West Virginia, 1870 US census)

Nancy Saucepan
Born Michigan c.1847 (Jackson, Michigan, 1870 US census)

Dagmar Sewer
(Female) Born c.1912
(Christiansted, Virgin Islands, 1930 US census)

Marmaduke Sewer
Married Mary Goulsbrough, St Paul, Lincoln, 11 June 1629

Dora Sideboard
Born 25 December 1891; died Port Allen,
Louisiana, USA, 15 October 1967

Ina Sink
Born 9 November 1877; died Kokomo,
Indiana, USA, April 1967

Yetta Sofa
Born St George in the East, London, 1886

Samuel Spoon
Married Anna Maria Aldred, St Peter Mancroft,
Norwich, Norfolk, 28 August 1858

Martha Kitchen Sunshine
Born West Ham, Essex, 1868

Benjamin Teapot
Born Neath, Glamorgan, 1858
*Two other boys born in Neath, in 1867 and 1878,
were given the same name.*

Dick Thickbroom
Baptized Church Gresley, Derbyshire, 27 July 1718

Thomas Toaster
Died Birmingham, Warwickshire, 1905

George T. Towel
Born Peckham, London, c.1900
(Peckham, 1900 England census)

Jessie T. Trolley
Born Wisbech, Cambridgeshire, c.1881
(Finchley, Middlesex, London, 1901 England census)
*Jessie T. Trolley's name was appropriate for her job – she was
listed in the 1901 census as a servant.*

Bendy Wall
Born Yarmouth, Norfolk, c.1851
(Great Yarmouth, 1861 England census)

Brick Wall
Born Kern, California, USA, 10 September 1964

Idadora Wall
Born Ohio c.1864 (Clark, Ohio, 1920 US census)

Ray Zerr
Born 7 January 1928; died Albany, Oregon, USA, June 1978

Comical Clothing

● ●

Chinchilla Belt
Born Maryland c.1852 (Anne Arundel,
Maryland, 1880 US census)

Caliopi Bikini
(Female) Born Greece c.1889; passenger on *Alice*, Patras,
Greece–New York, USA, arrived 26 May 1909

Esther Bonnet
Born South Dakota c.1912 (Beulah,
South Dakota, 1920 US census)

Wellington Boot
Born Linton, Cambridgeshire, 1869

Hattie Bowler
Married F. M. Starring, Kootenai,
Idaho, USA, 21 September 1910

Thomas Bowtie
Married Agnes Myller, St Andrew's,
Plymouth, Devon, 25 January 1613

Hattie Box
Born Texas c.1895 (Crockett, Texas, 1910 US census)

Minnie Boxers
Born Illinois 1897 (Colorado Springs,
Colorado, 1900 US census)

Cashmere Brassiere
Born Pennsylvania *c.*1874 (Westmoreland,
Pennsylvania, 1920 US census)

Bessie Youra Button
Married Robert Howard, Clay, Arkansas, USA, 4 October 1924

Panti Downey
Born North Carolina *c.*1865 (Sassafras Fork,
North Carolina, 1870 US census)

Ruby Slippers Doyle
Born Stockport, Cheshire, 2003

Welly Fun
Born China 1875 (Bergen, New Jersey, 1900 US census)

Sweater Glass
(Female) Born North Carolina 1899 (Jefferson,
North Carolina, 1900 US census)

Nylon Green
(Male) Born Nova Scotia, Canada, *c.*1877
(Houston, Texas, 1920 US census)
*He received the name 'Nylon' almost 60 years
before Nylon was invented.*

Beniventrus Hanky
Drowned while bathing, Chester, 6 August 1586
(Chester Coroners' Inquests)

Topsy Hatter
Born Rye, East Sussex, 1898

Knicker Hedwig
Born Texas c.1897 (San Angelo, Texas, 1930 US census)

Knickerbocker House
(Male) Born Indiana c.1874 (Anderson, Indiana, 1880 US census)

Jean Jacket
Born Ireland c.1837 (Paisley, Renfrewshire, 1841 Scotland census)

Levi Jeans
Baptized Stalbridge, Dorset, 24 February 1811
Levi Jeans was baptized over 60 years before Levi jeans were invented by Levi Strauss.

Velvet Jumper
Divorced San Diego, California, USA, 5 April 1982

Nick Kerr

Born 5 July 1884; died Columbia,
South Carolina, USA, January 1973

Alice Marie Rose Knicker

Born France *c*.1876 (City of London, 1911 England census)

Hugh Knicker

Born Ireland *c*.1866 (Maryhill,
Lanarkshire, 1871 Scotland census)

Brittany Knickerbocker

Born Stanislaus, California, USA, 14 February 1992

Theodosia Knickers

Born New York *c*.1848 (Oswego, New York, 1860 US census)

Annie Leggings

Born Leicestershire *c*.1872 (St George's Hanover Square,
London, 1901 England census)

Zip Lock

Married Dick Clayton, McNairy,
Tennessee, USA, 27 February 1895

Isaac Nylon

Married Harriet Townend, St Peter Southgate,
Norwich, Norfolk, 10 December 1845

Matilda Panter-Downes

Died Bristol, Gloucestershire, 1901

Jemima Panties

Born Poplar, London, *c*.1846 (Poplar, 1861 England census)

Elizabeth Pantoff
Married William Hutt, St Botolph without Bishopsgate,
London, 17 September 1751

Big Pants
(Male) Born c.1863 (Pine Ridge,
Dakota, 1886 US Indian census)

Leptimus Pants
Born Middlesbrough, Yorkshire, c.1872
(Oldham, Lancashire, 1911 England census)

Maria Panty
Born Leeds, Yorkshire, c.1845
(Church Fenton, Yorkshire, 1911 England census)

Moritz Pullover
Born Germany c.1836; passenger on Isaac Wright, Liverpool,
UK–New York, USA, arrived 18 March 1857

Anna Rack
Married St George in the East, London, 1881

Violet Sandals
Born Defford, Worcestershire, c.1886
(Cheltenham, Gloucestershire, 1911 England census)

T. Shirt
(Male) Born Ecclesfield, Yorkshire, 1843

Jim Shoe
Married Bawdrip, Somerset, 28 February 1602

Gross Shorts
Born 4 September 1916; died Miami,
Florida, USA, August 1985

Wilhelmina Sneakers
Born 16 November 1818; baptized Vizabapatam,
India, 29 November 1818

Bobby Socks
Born London c.1787
(Paddington, London, 1871 England census)

Cat Suit
Born Smyth, Virginia, USA, 12 July 1851

Nettie Sweater
Married Tank Louis, Holmes,
Mississippi, USA, 29 January 1908

Agnes Trainers
Born Siegen, Prussia, 4 December 1773

Augustas Trousers
Born Bloomsbury, London, c.1822
(Paddington, London, 1881 England census)

Lucy Trunks
Born Cardiff, Glamorgan, 1897

George Underwear
Born Texas c.1891 (Tarrant, Texas, 1910 US census)

Edmundes Wellies
Married Alicia Dentonne, Halifax, Yorkshire, 5 July 1562

Pants Winter
Born Finland c.1924; crew on *Randa*, Oslo,
Norway–New York, USA, arrived 5 August 1949

More Weird and Wonderful Names

●●●●●●●●●●●●●●●●●●●●●●●●

Lettice Agree
Born Mottram, Cheshire, c.1866 (Ashton-under-Lyne, Lancashire, 1871 England census)

Wow Ashworth
(Female) Born Lancashire c.1771 (Blackburn, Lancashire, 1841 England census)

Helen Back
Born Iowa c.1909 (Duncombe, Iowa, 1920 US census)

Piggy Banks
Born Kimmeridge, Dorset, c.1810
(East Stonehouse, Devon, 1851 England census)

Maybe Barnes
(Male) Born c.1661; died Middletown, Connecticut, America, 6 March 1748

Queen Goddess C. C. Davis-Ferdant Bartley
Born Nottingham 2001

Catharina Bendova
Died New York, USA, 16 January 1897

Cement Blackband
Died Aston, Warwickshire, 1895

Lili Blub
Born Philadelphia, Pennsylvania, USA, 20 November 1885

Okla Bobo
Born 19 December 1899; died Oklahoma City,
Oklahoma, USA, December 1968

Cicero Booboo
Born Alabama c.1854 (Limestone, Alabama, 1870 US census)

Waynard Bopp
Born 26 July 1899; died Chicago, Illinois, USA, January 1966

Ima Boy
Born c.1920 (Estillville, Virginia, 1930 US census)

Lamentation Brazille
Married David Loring, Hancock,
Georgia, USA, 25 January 1838

Romaine Bumb
Born 30 June 1913; died Lawrenceburg,
Indiana, USA, 18 October 2007

Hope Masie Burns
Born Cleveland 1994

Wood Burns
Born Louisiana c.1875 (Union, Louisiana, 1880 US census)

Orson Carter
Born Llanelly, Monmouthshire, 1905

Christian Charity
(Male) Baptized Hollesley, Suffolk, 19 December 1731

Alice Louisa Damp Child

Born Sandown, Hampshire, *c.*1877
(Portsea, Hampshire, 1891 England census)

Brookie Click

Born 4 May 1925; died Lawrence,
Kentucky, USA, 23 May 1990

Charles Cobweb

Baptized St James Roman Catholic Church, Winchester,
Hampshire, 12 February 1818

Clarence Cornelius Conrad Clockedile

Born 16 April 1913; died Yarmouth,
Maine, USA, 26 January 1986

Rich Cousins

Died Epping, Essex, 1851

Chris Cross

Born Ireland *c.*1872 (New York, 1910 US census)

Cosmo Crump

Born St George's Hanover Square, London, 1863

Manzy Crunk

Born 5 October 1901; died Killen, Alabama, USA, March 1975

Robert Morris Dancer

Born Prescot, Lancashire, 1903

Welcome Baby Darling

(Male) Born 17 October 1885; died Miami, Florida, USA, 9
December 1970

Darling Dear

(Male) Born South Carolina c.1807 (Newtown,
Mississippi, 1860 US census)

Encyclopedia Britannica Dewey

(Female) Born New York c.1819

*Encyclopedia Britannica Dewey did not like her first name
so went by the name Bitinia, Brittany or Britannia.
Her parents, Timothy and Beulah Dewey, also gave her
11 brothers and sisters strange names:*

Almira Melphomenia
Anna Diadama
Apeama
Armenius Philadelphus
Essephemia
Franklin Jefferson
Marcus Bonaparte
Octavia Ammonia
Philander Seabury
Pleiades Arastarcus
Victor Millenius

Tivoli Disharoon

Born 20 August 1894; died Salisbury,
Maryland, USA, September 1986

Prudentia Doolittle

Born c.1852; died Ormskirk, Lancashire, 1906

Primitive Dorbat

Born 28 June 1928; died Bridgeport,
Connecticut, USA, 20 May 2003

Maximina Dumdum
Born Balamban, Philippines, 1900; died
Balamban, 5 August 1981

I. Dunnit
(Female) Born Paisley, Renfrewshire, 9 October 1812

Blue Dye
Born Chesterfield, Derbyshire, 1986

Archibald Earthman
Born Dumfriesshire c.1840 (Lochmaben,
Dumfriesshire, 1841 Scotland census)

Alchemist-Jinade Leon D. Ellick
Born Waltham Forest, London, 2004

Himself Eubanks
Born 3 January 1892; died Augusta,
Georgia, USA, October 1976

Never Fail
(Male) Born Texas, USA, 30 June 1906; died Tulsa,
Oklahoma, June 1973

Will Fail
Born Texas, USA, 25 April 1893
(First World War draft registration)

Low Fee
Married Chorlton, Cheshire, 1908

John Whipple Filoon III
Born Onslow, North Carolina, USA, 6 April 1961

Last First
Born Florida, USA, 12 May 1907;
died Winter Haven, Florida, April 1982

Benny Fitt
Born Shoreditch, London, 1876

Festus Flipper
Born 15 November 1906; died Savannah,
Georgia, USA, 1 November 1996
His son (1933–92) was also called Festus Flipper.

Lentilhon Fluegge
Born 17 January 1895; died New York, USA, December 1981

Fanetta Fluke
Born Melksham, Wiltshire, 1867

Santee Foppee
Born 22 August 1901; died El Dorado, Arkansas,
USA, October 1967

Wonderful George Forsdyke
Born Bosmere, Suffolk, 1886

Scott Free
Born Ohio *c.*1897 (Paint, Ohio, 1930 US census)

Catherine Frisky
Born *c.*1826; died Uppingham, Rutland, 1907

Bada Funmaker
Born 19 December 1920; died Adams,
Wisconsin, USA, 4 November 1992

Strongman Fussell
Born Rochester, Kent, c.1821
(Newington, London, 1881 England census)

Amethyst Gallop
Born Winchester, Hampshire, 1919

Phil Gapp
Married Forehoe, Norfolk, 1859

Ann Clown Gentleman
Married St Pancras, London, 1880

John Giggler
Born Luton, Bedfordshire, c.1826 (Biggleswade,
Bedfordshire, 1861 England census)

Unique Glass
Born Oklahoma c.1903 (Oklahoma City, 1930 US census)

Will Gofar
Baptized Howden, Yorkshire, 15 January 1632

Lucinda Goodtime
Born Perry, Ohio, USA, 1884;
married Frank Houston, Perry, 1905

Alonzo Goody Goody
Born Sudbury, Suffolk, 1856

Brown Green
(Male) Born Gressenhall, Norfolk, c.1851
(Norwich, Norfolk, 1861 England census)

Grudgeworthy Grudgeworthy
(Female) Baptized Winkleigh, Devon, 21 February 1736

Cliff Hanger

Born Ohio c.1893 (McDonald, Ohio, 1910 US census)

Artificial Harris

Born 14 September 1884; died Little Rock,
Arkansas, USA, May 1971

B. Have

Born 26 August 1787; baptized St Mary's Independent,
Glossop, Derbyshire, September 1787

Viscount Heavican

Born Bury, Lancashire, 1890 (Bury, 1891 England census)
'Viscount' was his first name.

Miles High

Born Ulverston, Cumbria, 1847

X. Y. Z. Holyland

(Female) Born c.1851 (Thurlaston,
Leicestershire, 1851 England census)

Adeline Louisa Maria Horsey
de Horsey

Born London 24 December 1824; died Corby,
Northamptonshire, 25 May 1915

Ina Hurry

Born Arkansas c.1907 (Texarkana, Arkansas, 1930 US census)

Dorothea Mary A. E. Iceberg

Born City of London 1873

Ann Inch

Baptized St Kew, Cornwall, 16 February 1713

Successful Jackson

Married George Bell, Dallas, Texas, USA, 17 April 1989
*Their marriage was not successful, and they were
divorced on 15 May 1992.*

Leamonisha Iamunique Jenkins

Born Los Angeles, California, USA, 3 May 1990

Buster Journeycake

Born 23 May 1895; died Lawton,
Oklahoma, USA, March 1974

Wong Kee
(Female) Born China c.1874 (aboard ship *Glenlochy*,
Middlesbrough, Yorkshire, 1901 England census)

Lea King
(Female) Born Chard, Somerset, c.1777 (North Wraxall,
Wiltshire, 1861 England census)

Confidence Klotz
Born 1 August 1908; died Red Bluff,
California, USA, 4 August 2001

Shirley Knott
Born Edmonton, Middlesex, 1902

Ima Lady
Born 19 June 1916; died Morris,
Oklahoma, USA, 20 January 2005

Rich Lathers
Born South Carolina c.1870 (Fruit Cove,
Florida, 1910 US census)

Moses Lawn
Born Ireland c.1844 (Philadelphia,
Pennsylvania, 1870 US census)

Fossett Golden Legg
(Male) Married Melksham, Wiltshire, 1881

Licka Lick
(Male) Born France 1903; passenger on *La Bretagne*, Le Havre,
France–New York, USA, arrived 14 May 1906

Miles Long
Born Maine c.1846 (Bluehill, Maine, 1880 US census)

Noah Lott
Baptized Hipswell, Yorkshire, 16 August 1843

Despair Loveridge
Born Witham, Cambridgeshire, *c.*1857 (Little Paxton, Huntingdonshire, 1881 England census)

Bea Lowe
Baptized Winwick, Lancashire, 18 October 1706

Cuddles Lynn
Born 1 September 1936; died Glendale, California, USA, 6 March 2004

Winnie Mainprize
Born Tamworth, Staffordshire, 1910

Epaphroditus Marsh
Baptized Hannington, Wiltshire, 23 January 1636
His brothers were called Narcissus and Onesiphorus.

Patience Mayhem
Married William Vigian, Maidstone, Kent, 19 January 1596

Early Hawaiian McKinnon
Married Muriel Brown, Holmes, Florida, USA, 1934

Y. Mee
Born 1936; died Stoke-on-Trent, Staffordshire, 1997

Mary Mermaid
Baptized St Martin-in-the-Fields, London, 30 May 1690

George Washington Milkman
Married Chorlton, Lancashire, 1888

Annie Moment
Born Georgia *c.*1882 (Wrightsboro, Georgia, 1910 US census)

Mary Moon Moon
Born Clutton, Somerset, 1882

Helen Naughty Morton
Born 1906; died Hitchin, Hertfordshire, 1998

Arthur Mudlark
Born 18 December 1885; baptized Midsomer Norton,
Somerset, 10 January 1886
*Mudlarks were people – often children – who once scavenged
in the mud of riverbanks, such as those of the Thames in
London, searching for lost items they could sell.*

Magic Muxworthy
Born Doncaster, Yorkshire, 1889

Vera Necessary
Born 31 August 1922; died Tyler, Smith,
Texas, USA, 19 November 2001

May B. Nott
Born Illinois 1869 (Kewanne, Illinois, 1900 US census)

Y. Nott
(Female) Born 1930; died Tunbridge Wells, Kent, 2002

Marie Francoise Obscure
Baptized Lyons, France, 7 June 1817

Ann Other
Died Leyburn, Yorkshire, 1899

Joe Overthrow

Born Gloucester 1838

Faith Hope Charity Peace

Born Ashby-de-la-Zouch, Leicestershire, 1864

Perfect Perfect

Born Chatham, Kent, c.1887 (Chatham, 1891 England census)

Peter Piffle

Married Nancy Williams, Bourbon,
Kentucky, USA, 28 March 1798

Silver Pigg

Born 1 November 1923; died McCracken,
Kentucky, USA, 26 March 1989

Grace Pinkapank

Born 1 March 1909; died St Louis,
Missouri, USA, December 1974

William Plank A. Plank

Born Poole, Dorset, 1886

Liselotte Pook

Born 27 November 1904; passenger on *United States*,
Bremerhaven, Germany–New York, USA, arrived 20 March
1956; died Englewood, Colorado, June 1975

Anita Portfolio

Born New Jersey, USA, c.1910; passenger on *Vulcana*,
Naples, Italy–New York, arrived 28 July 1938

Lee Pover

Born Plymouth, Devon, 1959

Avast Price
Born 14 January 1919; died Monroe,
North Carolina, USA, April 1974

Fairest Price
(Male) Born North Carolina c.1904 (Duncan,
North Carolina, 1910 US census)

High Price
Married Presteigne, Herefordshire, 1861

John Lower Price
Born Wolverhampton, Staffordshire, 1844

Mad Price
(Male) Born Bishop Auckland, Durham, c.1865
(Bishop Auckland, 1891 England census)

Over Price
(Male) Born c.1812 (Merthyr Tydfil,
Glamorgan, 1841 Wales census)

Silly Price
(Female) Born Sheffield, Yorkshire, c.1855
(Sheffield, 1891 England census)

Irmgard Quapp
Passenger on *Zuiderkruis*, Rotterdam,
Netherlands–New York, USA, arrived 14 August 1956

Nathaniel Ratcatcher
Married Amye Wright, Stoke-by-Nayland, Suffolk, 23 July 1622

Iva Reason
Born 2 February 1876; died Farwell,
Michigan, USA, March 1967

Earthaline Revels
Born 29 October 1926; died San Francisco,
California, USA, 30 April 1996

Lynx Roadcap
(Male) Born Virginia c.1865 (Lineville,
Virginia, 1910 US census)

Susan Rottengoose
Baptized Hemsby, Norfolk, 10 July 1636

Pete Sake
Born Cheshire c.1840 (Macclesfield,
Cheshire, 1841 England census)

Elastic Scott
Died Montgomery, Alabama, USA, 28 December 1958

Great Scott
Born South Carolina c.1835 (Webster,
Georgia, 1870 US census)

Snooty Scott
Born Tennessee 1892 (Rutherford, Tennessee, 1900 US census)

Sufferance Scott
Born South Carolina c.1828 (Anderson,
South Carolina, 1850 US census)

Josiah Sinbody
Born Pennsylvania c.1836 (Yount, California, 1860 US census)

Lovie Slappy
Born c.1878 (Macon, Georgia, 1930 US census)

Postal Smalls
Born 9 October 1919; died Huger,
South Carolina, USA, 11 December 2008

Orange Snodgrass
Born 31 March 1894; died Fremont,
Nebraska, USA, June 1982

Mary Snogglegrass
Born Fife, c.1862 (St Giles-in-the-Fields,
London, 1881 England census)

Harriet Someone
Born 28 July 1884; died Miami, Florida, USA, November 1969

Ann Billion Sparkes
Married Shrewsbury, Shropshire, 1841

Satisfy Sparkes
Married John Lewis, Delaware, USA, 7 February 1809

Truelove Spark
(Male) Born Kentucky c.1831
(Morgan, Missouri, 1880 US census)

Lettice Spray
Baptized Greasley, Nottinghamshire, 23 April 1633

Elmadorus Nothing Sprinkle
Born Virginia, USA, c.1810; died March 1888

*Elmadorus Nothing Sprinkle, a hatter, had one daughter,
Memphis Tappon, with his first wife, and with his second,
Martha, née McCollum (born Scotland c.1833), two sons,
to whom they gave the strange names of Myrtle Ellmore and
Onyx Curren, and six daughters, Empress Vandalia, Tatnia Zain,
Okinna Maletta, Ogwilt, Agawith and Wintosse Emmah.*

Stan Still
Born Malling, Kent, 1901

William Short Story
Born Newcastle upon Tyne, Northumberland, 1846

Famous Stubblefield
Born Kentucky *c*.1903
(McCracken, Kentucky, 1910 US census)

Noah Tall
Baptized Antony, Cornwall, 21 April 1783

Thomas Teehee
Born Bilston, Staffordshire, *c*.1830
(Darlaston, Staffordshire, 1871 England census)

Annie Thing
Born Broughton, Buckinghamshire, *c*.1870
(Broughton, 1891 England census)

Silly Things
Born Stowmarket, Suffolk, c.1892
(Ipswich, Suffolk, 1901 England census)

William Thingy
Born Matlock, Derbyshire, *c*.1784
(Matlock, 1851 England census)

Virgil Toadvine
Born 13 February 1922; died Salisbury,
Maryland, USA, August 1980

Benoni Trampleasure
Born Kingsbridge, Devon, 14 February 1815

George Willard Pucker Tucker
Born Northumberland, Ontario, Canada, 30 May 1895

Matilda Jean Footprint Tustin
Born Cardiff, Glamorgan, 2004

Mercy Underling
Born Elham, Kent, 1882

Urho E. Wainionpoa
Born c.1908 (Quincy, Massachusetts, 1930 US census)
*In a court case, he claimed to be unable to work
because no one could remember his name.*

Love Wallops
(Female) Born Acton Turville, Gloucestershire, 1863

U. Watt
(Male) Married Castle Ward, Northumberland, 1900

Amelie What Watts
Married Marylebone, London, 1883

Nannie Wham
Born 7 April 1916; died Asheboro,
North Carolina, USA, April 1979

Little Green White
(Male) Born Texas c.1917 (Dewitt, Texas, 1920 US census)

Pearl E. White
Born Gravesend, Kent, 1908

Happy Always Wilkins
Born Dursley, Gloucestershire, 1849

Something Willis

(Male) Born Ireland c.1801 (Glamorgan, 1851 Wales census)

Auguste Wobble

Born c.1875; passenger on *Queen Elizabeth*, Southampton, UK–New York, USA, arrived 16 April 1947

Matthew Yellow Yellow

Born Thirsk, Yorkshire, 1862

Furry Youngman

Born 4 August 1896; died Ravenna, Ohio, USA, October 1979

School
Silliness

Henrietta Addition
Born Illinois c.1888 (Washington, DC, 1920 US census)

Junior Class
(Male) Born c.1924 (Randolph, Ohio, 1930 US census)

Ritta Desk
Born Missouri 1870 (St Louis, Missouri, 1900 US census)

Ann Eraser
Married John Mackie, Aberdeen, 13 May 1831

Ann Exam
Born Bristol, Gloucestershire, c.1805
(Edmonton, Middlesex, 1851 England census)

Pencil Farmer
Born Edgecombe, North Carolina, USA, 11 January 1928

Exam French
(Male) Born Oklahoma c.1907
(Alfalfa, Oklahoma, 1910 US census)

Charles Headmaster
Married Lambourn, Berkshire, October 1679

Crayola Hicks
Born 16 October 1935; died Butler,
Kentucky, USA, 25 May 2008

Frederick Alphabet Jones
Born Kendal, Westmorland, 1873

A. Level
Baptized Sudbury, Suffolk, 19 January 1792

Jim Locker
Married Stoke-on-Trent, Staffordshire, 1864

Geometry Middleton
Born c.1879; died Milwaukee,
Wisconsin, USA, 19 October 1974

Ida Pencil
Born Illinois *c.*1863 (Lincoln, Kansas, 1870 US census)

Fountain Penn
Born Virginia *c.*1834 (Mayo, Virginia, 1870 US census)

Comfort Satchel
Baptized Yevertoft, Northamptonshire, 1 November 1814

Gladys School
Born 31 December 1901; died Los Angeles,
California, USA, March 1978

Ink Smith
Married Whitby, Yorkshire, 1857

Abraham School House Stevens
Born Barking, Essex, *c.*1832 (Barking, 1871 England census)

Ima Teacher
Born *c.*1919 (Bexar, Texas, 1930 US census)

Ada Term
Born Walthamstow, Essex, *c.*1873
(Walthamstow, 1881 England census)

Ina Test
Born Illinois 1870 (Shelby, Tennessee, 1900 US census)

Potty Playtime

Batty Ball
(Female) Born North Meols, Lancashire, c.1797
(North Meols, 1871 England census)

Mark Foot Balls
Born South Shields, Durham, 1890

Teddy Bear
Born 1912; died Maidstone, Kent, 1998

Alley Bowling
(Male) Born Virginia c.1993
(Botecourt, Virginia, 1910 US census)

Raymond Gymnasium Brown
Resident of Brisbane, Queensland, Australia
(1936 Australian Electoral Roll)

Dylan Oxford United Collins
Born Oxford 1997

Bartholomew Cricket
Baptized St John, Margate, Kent, 25 April 1755

William Crossword
Died Hennepin, Minnesota, USA, 29 December 1914

Dan Darts
Born Biggleswade, Bedfordshire, 1874

Thomas Dodgem
Baptized Great Edstone, Yorkshire, 3 October 1774

Barb B. Doll
Born 25 September 1907; died Billings,
Montana, USA, June 1989

Cindy Doll
Married Dean Tvinnereim, Hennepin,
Minnesota, USA, 29 December 1984

Wanna Dolly
(Male) Born Lambeth, London, c.1864
(Lambeth, 1901 England census)

Cricket Fields
Born Kentucky 1896 (Forked Mouth,
Kentucky, 1900 US census)

William Footracer
Born Hamilton, Lanarkshire, c.1813
(Hamilton, 1871 Scotland census)

Sarah Bounce P. Frisby
Born Leicester 1878

Never Gamble
Born South Carolina c.1887 (Leesburg,
Florida, 1930 US census)

Bing Go
Born 10 May 1903; died Minneapolis,
Minnesota, USA, 6 June 1990

Henry Golf Green

Born 3 December 1899 (Hamilton, Tennessee,
USA, First World War draft registration)

Sport Model Higginbotham

Born 23 December 1941; died St Petersburg,
Florida, USA, 5 January 2009

Long Hop

Born China 1860 (New Orleans, Louisiana, 1900 US census)

Wendy House

Married Mark Smith, Swansea, Glamorgan, 1985

Harry Hurdler

Born Wokingham, Berkshire, 1866

Marathon Judge
Married Haydn Millard, Wycombe,
Buckinghamshire, April 1991

Harriet Circus Kirby
Born Skipton, Yorkshire, 1904

Kate Kite
Baptized Downend, Gloucestershire, 5 August 1883

Bowling Lane
(Male) Born Virginia c.1845 (Lickenhole,
Virginia, 1870 US census)

Modern Leggo
Born Penzance, Cornwall, 1859

Franz Netball
Born Wilfersdorf, Austria, 5 January 1867

Ping Pong
Born China c.1864 (San Francisco, California,
1910 US census)

Minnie Puzzle
Born Missouri c.1858 (Chillicothe, Missouri, 1880 US census)

Catherine Roundabout
Married John Cook, St Martin's, Birmingham,
Warwickshire, 29 December 1735

C. Saw
(Male) Born Edmonton, Middlesex, 1879

Lucy Skates
Baptized Winterbourne, Berkshire, 2 January 1780

Bob Sleigh

Baptized Edinburgh 6 November 1608

William Snooker

Married Ann Kerwood, Bosham, Sussex, 25 September 1775

Wii Tempest

Died Skipton, Yorkshire, 1851

Ferris Wheeler

Born Arkansas c.1898 (Van Buren, Arkansas, 1920 US census)
*The Ferris wheel was invented by George
Washington Gale Ferris in 1893.*

Golly Yoyo

Born Italy c.1860 (Schell Back, Nevada, 1880 US census)

Mind-boggling Music and Silly Sounds

MIND-BOGGLING MUSIC

Isabella Bugle
Baptized Christ Church, Tynemouth,
Northumberland, 18 July 1790

Harpyna Cymbal
Born 23 June 1896; died Los Angeles,
California, USA, 27 February 1982

Harry Rockett Drum
Born 1912; died Catawba,
North Carolina, USA, 2 August 1977

Honor Drum
Married Edmond Horele, London, 16 December 1720

Serious Drummer
Born 7 February 1872; died Atlanta,
Georgia, USA, December 1973

Dolly Greatsinger
Born Wisconsin c.1896 (Brooklyn,
Wisconsin, 1910 US census)

Music Hall
(Male) Born Aston, Warwickshire, c.1830
(Birmingham, Warwickshire, 1861 England census)

Melody Hummer
Born Los Angeles, California, USA, 15 October 1949

Epiphany Lullaby
Married Veryan, Cornwall, 3 January 1767

Rapper McBee
Born Ohio c.1881 (Sugar Creek, Ohio, 1930 US census)

Oral Musick
Born 3 March 1909; died Cedar Rapids,
Iowa, USA, 19 January 1993

Melody Musick
Born Hennepin, Minnesota, USA, 3 November 1951

Mel Oddy
Born Halifax, Yorkshire, 1886

Carrie Oke
Born Bideford, Devon, 1864

Piano Price
(Female) Born Arkansas c.1828 (Big Rock,
Arkansas, 1880 US census)

Isabel Ringer
Born Hartismere, Suffolk, 1911

Elsie Violin Sharp
Born Huddersfield, Yorkshire, 1891

Topsy Sharp
Born 10 March 1910; died Mineola,
Texas, USA, 12 September 1983

Rap Smith
Born Doncaster, Yorkshire, 1900

Sing Song
Died Liverpool, Lancashire, 1847

Rock Star
Born Italy 1886 (Jackson, Missouri, 1900 US census)

Priscilla Trumpet
Baptized Tipton, Staffordshire, 19 August 1832

Justin Tune
Born 20 December 1913; died
Miami, Florida, USA, 9 July 2002

I. Tunes
(Female) Married Durham 1874

SILLY SOUNDS
People whose surnames sound like noises . . .

● ● ● ● ● ● ● ● ● ● ●

Gideon Biff
Baptized Sherborne, Dorset, 14 April 1678

Bonnie Boing
Born c.1927 (Houma, Louisiana, 1930 US census)

Bing Bong
Born China 14 August 1874
(Vancouver, British Columbia, 1901 Canada census)

Didymus E. Buzz
Married Sarah Langley, Callaway,
Missouri, USA, 10 March 1839

Elizabeth Clang
Born Bury St Edmunds, Suffolk, 1845

Barnaby Crash
Married Anne Swinfield, St Mary's, Bedford, 10 July 1655

Charlotte Fizz
Born Falmouth, Cornwall, c.1827
(Cheltenham, Gloucestershire, 1901 England census)

John Glug
Baptized St George in the East, London, 25 June 1730

Lambert Jangle
Born Pennsylvania 1891 (Nesquehoning,
Pennsylvania, 1900 US census)

Walter Jingle
Married Ellen Sedgwick, Wortley, Yorkshire, 1919

Theodor Miaow
Born Schwaan, Germany, 26 August 1832

Luscrestin Oink
(Female) Born Illinois c.1898 (Chicago,
Illinois, 1910 US census)

Annie Pow
Born Bitton, Gloucestershire, 25 June 1848

Hildegarde K. Quack
Born Birkenhead, Cheshire, 1914

Lester G. Sizzle
Born Muhlenburg, Kentucky, USA, 11 May 1923

Leah Slosh
Born Whitechapel, London, 1873

Best Splat
Married Mary Langworthy, Whitestone, Devon, 13 April 1691

Richard Cleland Squark
Born Totnes, Devon, 1892

Frances Squeal
Married John Blake, St Philip, Charleston,
South Carolina, USA, 28 December 1771

Augustus Swish
Born Hackney, London, *c*.1875
(Hackney, 1881 England census)

Sophia Thud
Baptized St Mary, Stamford, Lincolnshire, 26 August 1828

Alexander Thwack
Born Middlesex *c*.1827 (Holborn,
London, 1851 England census)

Madeleine Twang
Married Lambeth, London, 1877

Cornelius Whizz
Born New Jersey, *c*.1902 (Butler, New Jersey, 1910 US census)

Cleopatra Woosh
Married William Arnold, Clay, Missouri, USA, 11 June 1872

Samuel Zap
Married Elizabeth Ludlom, South Wingfgield,
Derbyshire, 16 July 1785

Philopena Zing
Born Germany *c*.1806 (Baltimore, Maryland, 1870 US census)

Lilly Zoom
Born Brantham Essex, *c*.1863
(Ipswich, Suffolk, 1881 England census)

Batty Battles and Crackpot Criminals

BATTY BATTLES

Ann Ambush
Born Maryland c.1825 (Newburyport, Massachusetts, 1870 US census)

Goldie Ambush
Born 10 November 1901; died District of Columbia, USA, 9 March 1992

Bertram Canon Ball
Born Stourbridge, Worcestershire, 1875

Wealthy Battle
(Female) Born Georgia c.1915 (Macon, Georgia, 1920 US census)

Fred Bigsoldier
Born Nebraska c.1870 (Perkins, Oklahoma, 1930 US census)

Barry Cade
Married Jean M. Handley, Peterborough, Northamptonshire, 1995

Peculiar Cannon
(Female) Born Claypole, Lincolnshire, *c*.1876
(Hawton, Nottinghamshire, 1881 England census)

Bomb Gibson
Born Currie, Midlothian, *c*.1838
(Dunfermline, Fife, 1881 Scotland census)

Tommy Gun
Born Evesham, Worcestershire, 1838

James Golden Gunn
Married Isle of Wight 1856

Ray Gunn
Born 3 August 1930; died Orlando,
Florida, USA, 12 December 1988

Rifle Handworker
Born Russia *c*.1851 (Leeds, Yorkshire, 1891 England census)

Tom A. Hawk
Born St Dennis, Cornwall, *c*.1890
(St Dennis, 1891 England census)

Bullet Head
Born California *c*.1850 (Martins Ferry,
California, 1880 US census)

Norman Knight
Born Elland, Yorkshire, 15 August 1887

Flint Lock
Born Alabama *c*.1908 (Houston, Alabama, 1930 US census)

Perry Manywounds
Born 25 August 1926; died Sioux,
North Dakota, USA, 23 June 1994

Lodewycke Massacre
Married Jane Vreeland, Bergen,
New Jersey, USA, 2 August 1833

Dinah Might
Born Ventura, California, USA, 30 November 1956

Rick O'Shea
Married Kennington, London, 1864

Grenade Parson
Born 18 February 1910; died Detroit,
Michigan, USA, July 1989

Dynamite Partee
Born North Carolina *c.*1900 (Winston-Salem,
North Carolina, 1930 US census)

Warren Peace
Born New York *c.*1866 (Essex, New York, 1880 US census)

What Peace
Born Huddersfield, Yorkshire, 1854

Nancy Shotgun
Born 16 November 1973; died Fremont,
Wyoming, USA, 14 June 2008

Sniper Snodgrass
Born Vermont *c.*1884 (Clark, Wisconsin, 1910 US census)

Crusher Thrailkill

Born 20 April 1938; died Hennepin,
Minnesota, USA, 20 March 1995

Des Troyer

Born 9 April 1888; died Goshen, Indiana, USA, February 1979

Thomas Weapon

Married Mary Dearling, Bosham, Sussex, 15 September 1674

Pistol Pete Wiley

Born Tennessee c.1917 (Henry, Tennessee, 1920 US census)

Sword Wilkinson

(Male) Born Holmfirth, Yorkshire, c.1845
(Dewsbury, Yorkshire, 1881 England census)

CRACKPOT CRIMINALS
• • • • • • • • • • • • • • • • •

Robin Banks

Born Georgia c.1845 (Fayette, Georgia, 1870 US census)

Rob Bery

Born Whitechapel, London, 1857

Pirate Black

Born 3 August 1922; died San Francisco,
California, USA, 2 April 2006

Fred Burglar

Born c.1900; died Greensboro,
North Carolina, USA, 4 July 1922

Able Crook
Born North Carolina c.1866 (Buncombe,
North Carolina, 1870 US census)

Justa Crook
(Female) Born London c.1855
(Mile End, London, 1901 England census)

Young Crook
Born Highworth, Wiltshire, 1843

Soapy Crooks
Married Bosmere, Suffolk, 1891

Doris Diddle
Born 13 July 1921; died Columbiana,
Ohio, USA, 24 October 2002

Apalize Fightmaster
Married Preston L. McHatton, Grant,
Kentucky, USA, 13 April 1851

Robber Gotcher
Born Texas c.1863 (Collin, Texas, 1880 US census)

Job Gunman
Born Connecticut c.1878 (Stonington,
Connecticut, 1880 US census)

Wolff Hangman
Born Russia c.1839 (Mile End, London, 1901 England census)

Double Killer
Born Alberta c.1858 (Macleod, Alberta, 1911 Canada census)

Pirate King
Born Missouri c.1835 (Richmond, Missouri, 1880 US census)

Burglar McMillon
Born Virginia *c*.1873 (Snow Creek, Virginia, 1880 US census)

Nick Money
Born 22 November 1891; died Fort Recovery,
Ohio, USA, December 1972

Mary Murder
Baptized Elsworth, Cambridgeshire, 13 September 1846

Tiny Outlaw
(Female) Born *c*.1913 (Early, Georgia, 1930 US census)
Tiny was the daughter of Handy Outlaw.

Robbort [*sic*] Robbing Overcash
Born North Carolina *c*.1913 (Granite Falls,
North Carolina, 1930 US census)

Dawn Raid
Married Dragan Radosavljevich, Islington,
London, September 1996

Jack Ripper
Born Kentucky *c*.1865 (Short Creek, Kentucky,
1910 US census)

Jack D. Ripper
Born *c*.1921 (Portland, Oregon, 1930 US census)

John A. Robber
Born Pennsylvania *c*.1851 (Turbett,
Pennsylvania, 1860 US census)
Nine-year-old John A. Robber was the sister of
Mary A. Robber (aged five).

Anna Sasin
Born Austria *c*.1882 (Clayton, Michigan, 1910 US census)

Stanley Slaughter Slaughter
Born Aylsham, Norfolk, 1893

Murder John Smith
Born St George's Hanover Square, London, 1878

Eunice Strangler
Born Kansas *c*.1901 (Sharon, Kansas, 1920 US census)

Daily Swindle
Born 28 May 1917; died Toledo, Ohio, USA, 26 February 1983

Hans Up
Born 15 April 1722; baptized Sodra Melby,
Kristianstad, Sweden, 15 April 1722; died 4 February 1728

Mad
Moves

● ● ● ● ● ● ● ● ● ● ● ● ● ● ● ● ● ● ●

Ryan Air
Born Northumberland 1992

Caroline Airline
Born South Carolina c.1850 (Reeves,
South Carolina, 1880 US census)

May Fly Away
Born 1896 (Fort Berthold, 1896 US Indian census)

Submarine Miners Banacks
Born Kingston upon Hull, Yorkshire, c.1837
(Kingston upon Hull, 1891 England census)

Ferrari Porsche Beard
Born Reading, Berkshire, 1998

Mercedes Bentley
Born c.1899 (Douglas, Arizona, 1930 US census)

Mercedes Bentz
Born c.1927 (Verdigris, Oklahoma, 1930 US census)

Minnie Bike
Born Michigan c.1863 (Mason, Michigan, 1880 US census)

Rhoda Boat
Born Rogate, Hampshire, c.1813
(Graffham, Sussex, 1861 England census)

Driver Bus
(Male) Born Somerset c.1879
(Leeds, Yorkshire, 1901 England census)

Darby Caravan
Married Mary Frazier, St James Duke's Place,
London, 8 January 1694

Henry Ford Carlock
Born USA c.1922; crew on *Michael James Monohan*,
Eniwetok, Marshall Islands–San Francisco, California,
USA, arrived 31 August 1945

Ford Carr
Born Newcastle upon Tyne, Northumberland, c.1863
(Newcastle upon Tyne, 1871 England census)

Parker Carr
Baptized Horsted Keynes, Sussex, 5 November 1865

Car Chase
Born Brook, Hampshire, *c*.1858 (Titchfield,
Hampshire, 1881 England census)

Minnie Cooper
Born Spalding, Lincolnshire, 1859

Leicester Railway Cope
Baptized Normanton Temple, Derbyshire, 23 August 1863

Laurie Driver
Born 1895; died Surrey 1990

Wealthy Driver
Born Alabama *c*.1853 (Young, Texas, 1880 US census)

Wanda Farr
Born Indiana *c*.1904 (Indianapolis, Indiana, 1910 US census)

Penny Farthing
Born England *c*.1815 (Gravesend, New York, 1860 US census)

Erastus K. Fillerup
Married Lillian Teterson, Idaho Falls,
Idaho, USA, 30 October 1924

George Garage
Born Salford, Lancashire, *c*.1858
(Salford, 1871 England census)

Georgiana Top Gear
Born Wambrook, Somerset, *c*.1862 (Tarrant Hinton,
Dorset, 1891 England census)

Low Gear
Born c.1921 (Gilkey, North Carolina, 1930 US census)

Lamborghini Cheyenne Holcomb
Born Harlan, Kentucky, USA, 23 January 1996

Wooden Hull
(Male) Baptized Norfolk, Connecticut, USA, 2 July 1800
He was one of several generations of Wooden Hulls.

Local Freight Johnson
Born Henderson, North Carolina, USA, 18 June 1911;
died Henderson 12 June 1959

Ria Light
Born Portsmouth, Hampshire, 1994

Victoria Line
Born Texas c.1885 (Monclova, Ohio, 1920 US census)

Porsche Mercedes Lockwood
Born Warwickshire 1995

Rhoda Long
Baptized Guiseley, Yorkshire, 18 August 1764

Rolla Long
(Male) Born Texas c.1905
(Tulare, California, 1910 US census)

Mary Moped
Born c.1816 (Barton Regis,
Gloucestershire, 1841 England census)

Lucia de Bustinzuria Omnibus

Married Matheo de Ybasseta, San Pedro Apostol, Berriatua,
Vizcaya, Spain, 3 June 1653

*The first buses, which were drawn by horses, were called
omnibuses, from the Latin for 'for all', because any
member of the public could travel in them.*

Awful Parker

Born Tennessee *c.*1859 (Dyer, Tennessee, 1880 US census)

Laurie Pickup

Married Rochdale, Lancashire, 1853

L. Plate

(Female) Born Sussex *c.*1811 (Warminghurst,
Sussex, 1841 England census)

Noel Plate
Born Binfield, Buckinghamshire, c.1847
(Hendon, Middlesex, 1891 England census)

George Puffpuff
Born Illinois c.1866 (Monroe, Illinois, 1870 US census)

Putt Putt
(Male) Born Ohio c.1879 (Marion, Ohio, 1880 US census)

John Railway
Born Elham, Kent, c.1862 (Elham, 1911 England census)

Limousine Reese
Born 1 March 1917; died Chesapeake,
Virginia, USA, 10 April 2002

Joy Rider
(Male) Born Missouri 1895 (Kansas City,
Missouri, 1900 US census)

Royce Rolls
Born Oxford 1944

Rolls Royse
Born Massachusetts, USA, 3 March 1883; died Shasta,
California, 30 August 1968

Lucious P. Van Scooter
Born New York c.1841 (Hornellsville,
New York, 1880 US census)

Porsche Carrera Scott
Born St Albans, Hertfordshire, 1989

Rick Shaw
Born Romford, Essex, c.1857 (Tottenham,
London, 1881 England census)

Maude Ship
Born London c.1866 (Hackney, London, 1901 England census)
She had a daughter, another Maude Ship, born c.1892.

Max Speed
Born Louth, Lincolnshire, 1861

Christopher Tooslow
Married Elinor Walter, St Martin's, Exeter,
Devon, 23 December 1645

Urban Walk
Born c.1918 (Newburyport, Massachusetts, 1930 US census)

Frederick Careless Walker
Born Westmorland 1902

Risky Walker
Born Harrington, Cumberland, c.1880
(Parton, Cumberland, 1880 census)

Slack Walker
Born Wigton, Cumberland, 1840

Cycle Ward
Born 1 February 1905; died Pulaski,
Tennessee, USA, November 1969

William Whitevan
Born Farnhill, Yorkshire, c.1807
(Farnhill, 1871 England census)

Proposterous Places

AROUND THE COMPASS

North East
(Male) Born 21 January 1715; baptized St Mary the Virgin
Aldermanbury, London, 25 January 1715

West North
(Male) Born Missouri c.1862 (St Louis,
Missouri, 1880 US census)

East South
(Male) Born c.1815 (Portland,
Oregon Territory, 1850 US census)

South West
(Male) Born Chillacothe, Missouri, USA, 15 May 1852

Percy Stonehenge W. Ansell
Born St Olave'S, Southwark, London, 1874

Sandy Beach
(Female) Born St George in the East, London, c.1899
(St George in the East, 1901 England census)

Atlantic Ocean Beals
Married Carey Bradfield, Randolph,
Indiana, USA, 8 January 1836

Big Ben
Born California c.1835 (Lincoln, California, 1880 US census)

Mont Blanc
Born c.1806; died Huddersfield, Yorkshire, 1881

London Bridge
Born North Carolina c.1848 (Jefferson,
Missouri, 1870 US census)

Africa Bush
Born Virginia c.1863 (Portsmouth, Virginia, 1870 US census)

Windsor Castle
Born Radford, Nottinghamshire, 1876

Nelson Column
Born 12 June 1899 (Nacogdoches,
Texas, USA, First World War draft registration)

Hampton Court
Born Wandsworth, London, 1868

Phila Delphia
Born Cornwall 1840 (Buryan, Penwith,
Cornwall, 1841 England census)

Sarah Desert
Baptized St Leonard's, Shoreditch, London, 1 April 1804

Sandy Dune
Born 23 December 1952; died Barstow,
California, USA, 4 September 2000

Cliff Edge
Born Haslingden, Lancashire, 1903

Ireland England
(Female) Born Kentucky c.1896
(Abbott, Kentucky, 1910 US census)

London England
Born 26 January 1914; died Troy,
Michigan, USA, 9 November 1989

Merry England
Born Michigan, USA, 30 June 1953; died Los Angeles,
California, 1 May 1988

Paddy Fields
Born West Derby, Lancashire, 1908

Sherwood Forest
Born Blackpool, Lancashire, c.1891
(Waventree, Lancashire, 1901 England census)

Paris France
(Male) Born Missouri c.1892 (Clark, Missouri, 1910 US census)

Robert The France
Born 12 November 1948; died Northville,
New York, USA, January 1980
*He is one of many people who have
'The' as one of their names.*

United States Freeland
(Female) Born Missouri c.1838 (Washington,
Kansas, 1910 US census)

Boston Frog
Resident of Patapsco, Maryland (1790 US census)

Greenland Greenland
(Male) Born Ohio 1900 (Marion, Ohio, 1900 US census)

Albert Hall
Baptized St Martin-in-the-Fields, London, 26 October 1600

Sydney Harbour
Born Chesterfield, Derbyshire, 1909

America Icenoggle
Born Huntsville, Illinois, USA, 13 March 1859;
died 28 September 1934

England Ireland
(Male) Born Liverpool c.1854
(Everton, Lancashire, 1861 England census)

River Jordan
Baptized English Bicknor, Gloucestershire, 16 November 1766

Scot Land
Born Kentucky c.1891 (Butler, Ohio, 1920 US census)

Sahara Lara
Born 23 August 1917; died Rancho Cucamonga,
California, USA, 3 July 2002

Luther Denmark Longbottom
(Male) Born Silsden, Yorkshire, c.1848
(Silsden, 1881 England census)

Asia Minor
Born Pennsylvania 1881 (Monongahela Township,
Pennsylvania, 1900 US census)

Daisy Deepsea Mitchell
Born Edmonton, Middlesex, 1890

Rocky Mountain
Born Alamada, California, USA, 22 October 1922;
died Paradise, California, 25 October 2002

Ben Nevis
Born France *c*.1845 (St Mary in the Castle,
Hastings, Sussex, 1871 England census)

Hyde Park
Died Kensington, London, 1864

World Peek
(Male) Born Georgia *c*.1903 (Polk, Georgia, 1910 US census)

Dusty Rhodes
Born 1940; died Wigan, Lancashire, 1999

Heath Roe
(Male) Born Nottingham *c*.1836
(Nottingham, 1841 England census)

Hilarious Rome
Born 24 July 1932; died Tucson, Arizona, USA, March 1987

Wooloomooloo Roscoe
(Male) Born Oldham, Lancashire, 1876
*Woolloomooloo (with two ls) is a suburb of Sydney,
New South Wales, Australia.*

Arctic Jack Seerock
Born *c*.1903 (Chandalar, Alaska Territory, 1930 US census)

C. Side
(Female) Born St Saviour, Southwark, London, 1841

America Sparrow
Born Virginia c.1818 (Norfolk, Virginia, 1850 US census)

Himalaya Squance
Born Wilcove Anthony, Cornwall, c.1856

Victoria Station
Born North Carolina c.1842 (Edgecombe,
North Carolina, 1870 US census)

Eiffel Tower Sutherland
(Female) Born Indiana c.1895 (Marion,
Indiana, 1920 US census)

James Afghanistan Tomblin
Born Leigh, Lancashire, 1880

Angelo Volcano
Born Italy c.1878; passenger on *Republic*, Naples, Italy–
Boston, Massachusetts, USA, arrived 22 March 1904

Ocean Wave
(Female) Born Humboldt, California, USA, 12 November 1974

Ally Way
Born Saddleton, Surrey, 1961

Isla White
Born London c.1846 (Aveley, Essex, 1851 England census)

Holly Wood
Born Faversham, Kent, 1901

UNITED STATES

The names of some of the 50 states of the United States, such as Virginia, Carolina and Georgia, are often used as personal names. There are also famous fictitious characters, from Indiana Jones to Hannah Montana, whose names include state names, but some of those that follow are even more inventive – some may take a bit of thinking about.
See if you can work them all out . . .

Nev Ada
(Female) Born Kansas *c.*1870 (Oklahoma, USA, 1890 Oklahoma census)

M. Aine
(Male) Born Spain *c.*1828 (New York, 1860 US census)

Al Aska
Born 5 November 1901; died New York, USA, August 1955

Allie Bama
Born Texas *c.*1898 (Blossom, Texas, 1910 US census)

Missouri Amazon Barnett
(Female) Born Texas *c.*1858 (Upshur, Texas, 1880 US census)

Rhode Island Bartholomew
(Female) Born Indiana 1854 (Franklin, Indiana, 1880 US census)

South Dakota Carter
Born Florida *c.*1893; died Manatee, Florida, USA, May 1965

New Mexico Chapman

(Female) Born Kentucky c.1914 (Pond Fork,
Kentucky, 1920 US census)
*New Mexico had an older sister called Nebraska,
born in Kentucky c.1908.*

Boston Massachusetts Day

Born Wilkes, North Carolina, USA, 4 November 1907

Mich Egan

Born Ireland 1866 (Manhattan, New York, 1900 US census)

Pennsylvania Flag

(Female) Born Tennessee c.1902 (Haywood,
Tennessee, 1910 US census)

Cali Fornia

Born Arizona c.1886 (Seattle, Washington, 1910 US census)

New York Henry

Born Louisiana c.1867 (De Soto, Louisiana, 1870 US census)

O. Hio

(Female) Born New York c.1847 (Fulton,
New York, 1910 US census)

Ida Ho

Born New York c.1877 (Buffalo, New York, 1880 US census)

Oakley Homer

Born West Virginia c.1859 (Gallipolis, Ohio, 1930 US census)

Hawaii Huq

Born Cardiff, Glamorgan, 1964

George Ia
Born Oldbury, Worcestershire, c.1864
(Oldbury, 1891 England census)

Louis Iana
Born Italy c.1883 (Luzerne, Pennsylvania, 1910 US census)

Clinton Illinois
Born Jerome, Ohio, USA, 7 February 1879;
died Inlet, Washington, USA, 28 April 1956

Carol Ina
Born Harris, Texas, USA, 23 March 1960

I. Owa
(Male) Born Hawaii c.1901 (Kaapoko,
Hawaii, 1910 US census)

Mrs Ippi
Mathilda, wife of Michael Ippi, born Hungary 31 December
1880; died South Amboy, New Jersey, USA, February 1977

George R. Kansas
Born Arkansas c.1902 (Whitley, Arkansas, 1920 US census)

Indiana Kettle
Born Dudley, Staffordshire, 1854

Mary Land
Baptized Taynton, Gloucestershire, 2 February 1599

Connecticut Nixon
(Female) Born Georgia c.1864
(Ty Ty, Georgia, 1920 US census)

Carolina North
Baptized St Phillip's, Birmingham,
Warwickshire, 16 April 1759

Dakota North
Born Harrison, Kentucky, USA, 11 February 1997

Flo Rider
Born 12 March 1923; died York,
Pennsylvania, USA, 15 November 1998

Carolina South
Born Lambeth, London, c.1874
(Camberwell, London, 1881 England census)

Minnie Sowter
Born Mansfield, Nottinghamshire, 1893

Missouri Stew
(Female) Born Louisiana c.1850
(Natchitoches, Louisiana, 1880 US census)

Oregon Strong
Born 26 July 1918; died Dallas,
Texas, USA, 11 December 1964

Curly Tennessee
Born Shalford, Essex, c.1887
(West Ham, Essex, 1891 England census)

Ken Tuckey
Born 22 June 1916; died Naugatuck,
Connecticut, USA, 30 April 1997

New Jersey Ward
(Male) Born New Jersey c.1856
(Gloucester, New Jersey, 1860 US census)

Della Ware
Born 27 October 1889; died Saegertown,
Pennsylvania, USA, February 1969

D. C. Washington
Born 13 July 1903; died Monroe,
Louisiana, USA, 27 April 1991

South Carolina Washington
(Female) Born Texas c.1865 (Jones Prairie,
Texas, 1880 US census)

Virginia West
Born Virginia c.1820 (Norfolk, Virginia, 1870 US census)

Harry Zona
Born 26 August 1901; died Ellwood City,
Pennsylvania, USA, May 1974

Utah Zumwait
Born 4 July 1899; died Bountiful, Utah, USA, 19 May 1998

Perfect Pairs

It is not that uncommon for people whose names fit well together to end up getting married. In the United States, women often keep their original names and add on that of their husband, so when Mary Hammer married Andrew Nail, she might be known as Mary Hammer Nail. In the UK, women more often give up their surnames on marriage, so the last time the two surnames will be seen together is on the wedding invitation.

● ●

Aston–Martin
Karen N. Aston married Jonathan R. Martin, York, 1997

Axe–Killer
William Axe married Mary Killer, Ashbourne,
Derbyshire, 1914

Bacon–Roll
Annie Bacon married Oliver Roll, Wandsworth,
London, June 2003

Batty–Ball
Fred Batty married Clara J. Ball,
Ashton-under-Lyne, Lancashire, 1915

Beach–Ball
John Beach married Jane Ball, St Pancras,
London, 16 August 1825

Beard–Shaver

Harriet Beard married Madison Shaver, Rowan,
North Carolina, USA, 25 December 1865

Bell–Bottoms

William S. Bell married Barbara A. Bottoms,
Chester-le-Street, Durham, 1912

Bird–Brain

George Isaac Bird married Alice Brain,
Bristol, Gloucestershire, 25 December 1890

Bird–Nest

John Bird married Margaret Nest, Hopton
Wafers, Shropshire, 6 May 1810

Black–White
Robert Black married Marthy White, Maury,
Tennessee, USA, 2 March 1819

Bow–Arrow
Dorothy Bow married Richard Arrow, Oldstock,
Massachusetts, USA, 13 July 1801

Brain–Box
Jemima Brain married William Box,
Shipston-on-Stour, Warwickshire, 1912

Bull–Bush
Frederick C. Bull married Emma E. Bush,
Shoreditch, London, 1915

Butcher–Baker
Joseph Butcher married Martha Baker,
Crewkerne, Somerset, 1 June 1803

Cannon–Ball
Ann Cannon married John Ball, St Saviour's,
Southwark, London, 1830

Carr–Driver
Tommie Levada Carr married Jemmy Ray Driver,
Putnam, Tennessee, USA, 23 December 1967

Carr–Park
David H. Carr married Ethel F. Park,
Barrow-in-Furness, Cumbria, 1913

Cat–Dog
John Cat married Bessie Dog, Bennett,
South Dakota, USA, 29 May 1921

Cock–Roach
Hannah Cock married Thomas Roach,
Burnley, Lancashire, 1912

Dailey–Exam
Daniel Dailey married Margaret Exam,
St George in the Borough, London, 31 December 1782

Day–Light
Elizabeth M. Day married Albert F. Light,
Edmonton, Middlesex, 1919

Fish–Pye
Elizabeth Fish married Charles Pye, Bolton, Lancashire, 1927

Flower–Power
Carl E. V. Flower married Rebecca B. J. Power,
Dudley, West Midlands, 1996

Good–Bye
Robert Good married Elizabeth Bye, Haywood,
Tennessee, USA, 8 July 1963

Goody–Goody
Jill E. Goody married David D. Goody, Halifax, Yorkshire, 1986

Hammer–Nail
Mary Hammer married Andrew Jackson Nail,
Shelby, Texas, USA, 1839

Hand–Baggs
William G. Hand married Mildred Baggs,
Wimborne, Dorset, 1925

Hand–Foot
Rhoda Hand married Stephen Foot, Fair Haven,
Connecticut, USA, 25 March 1795

Handy–Cappe
William Handy married Anne Cappe, Butlers Marston,
Warwickshire, 26 October 1803

Hare–Brain
Deborah K. Hare married Ian M. Brain,
Halifax, Yorkshire, 1988

High–Price
Beatrice High married Frederick Price,
Wandsworth, London, 1919

Hunny–Bear
Hugh Hunny married Susanna Bear, St Endellion,
Cornwall, 11 February 1701

James–Bond
John James married Margaret Bond,
Chesterfield, Derbyshire, 1913

King–Kong
Jeremy B. King married Rosalyn L. Kong,
Sodbury, Gloucestershire, 1989

Large–Butt
Lottie L. Large married Francis H. Butt,
Cirencester, Gloucestershire, 1913

Lea–King
Annie Lea married George King, Birkenhead, Cheshire, 1915

Leak–Tapp
Sarah Leak married Steven Tapp, Thanet, Kent, 1993

Little–Large
Kathleen Little married George Large,
Bristol, Gloucestershire, 1921

Lock–Key
Hannah Lock married Richard Key,
Covent Garden, London, 31 May 1800

Long–Short
William A. Long married Nancy Gentry Short, Vernon,
Missouri, USA, 22 August 1877

Low–Price
Obadiah Low married Elisabeth Price, Kidderminster,
Worcestershire, 28 December 1723

Marks–Spencer
Elsabeth [sic] Marks married Miss Emma Spencer, Clinton,
Missouri, USA, March 1898

May–Pole
Deborah May married Keith Pole,
Pontefract, Yorkshire, August 2005

McDonald–Burger
Frederick McDonald married Elizabeth Burger,
New York, USA, 1793

Money–Penny
Ernest J. Money married Annie S. Penny,
Chorlton, Lancashire, 1922

Moore–Less
Dorothy Moore married Samuel Less,
St Marylebone, London, 1921

Morris–Dance
Nora M. Morris married Francis D. Dance,
Basford, Nottinghamshire, 1919

Needle–Cotton
Gary J. W. Needle married Samantha L. Cotton,
Rochdale, Lancashire, 2002

Night–Day
George Night married Susan Day, Whitley,
Kentucky, USA, 4 June 1820

Quack–Quack
Margaret E. Quack married Harold H. K. Quack,
Liverpool, Lancashire, 1913

Rich–Poor
Henry Rich married Elizabeth Poor, Boston,
Massachusetts, America, 1 October 1705

Ring–Bell
Elizabeth M. Ring married Matthew D. Bell,
Todmorden, Yorkshire, 1997

Rollings–Stone
Andrea Rollings married Stephen J. Stone,
St Austell, Cornwall, 1991

Rude–Bottom
Andrew O. Rude married Jean E. Bottom,
Riverside, California, USA, 7 June 1969

Sargeant–Major
Edwin Sargeant married Catherine R. Major,
Brentford, Middlesex, 1912

Sargent–Pepper
Charles Sargent married Lucy Pepper,
Aston, Warwickshire, 1916

Seymour–Bottom
William Seymour married Jane Bottom,
Wandsworth, London, 1912

Shepherd–Pye
Mark A. Shepherd married Astrid R. Pye,
Canterbury, Kent, 1993

Sherlock–Holmes
John Sherlock married Florence Holmes,
Wolstanton, Staffordshire, 1921

Short–Tall
Jane Short married John Tall,
Winchester, Hampshire, 21 January 1832

Silver–Gold
Mark Silver married Bernice Gold, Redbridge, Essex, 1994

Snow–Ball
Experience Snow married Thomas Ball,
Marlborough, Massachusetts, America, 12 July 1749

Snow–Mann
Florence M. Snow married Conrad A. Mann,
Tendring, Essex, 1919

Summers–Day
George C. Summers married Rosetta Day,
Colchester, Essex, 1918

Sun–Tan
Jian H. Sun married Koi E. Tan,
Lewes, East Sussex, 2003

Trimmer–Hedges
Fanny Trimmer married Charles Hedges,
Tring, Hertfordshire, 28 November 1891

Wall–Flower
George Wall married Sarah Flower, Langar Cum Barnston,
Nottinghamshire, 11 October 1714

Warren–Peace
Alison Warren married Andrew J. Peace,
Chichester, West Sussex, 2000

White–Wash
David White married Deborah Wash, Thurrock, Essex, 1987

Wild–Bull
Ann Wild married Joseph Bull,
Chatteris, Cambridgeshire, 25 July 1793

Winter–Spring
Stephen Winter married Wendy Spring,
Pontypool, Monmouthshire, 1992

Wise–Guy
George Wise married Daisy Guy, Fulham, London, 1915

Whyte–Pants

Joyce Whyte married Rogar [*sic*] Pants,
Allhallows London Wall, 7 October 1652

Wolf–Fox

George Wolf married Elizabeth Fox,
Humberstone, Leicestershire, 30 November 1773

Wright–Wong

Billy D. Wright married Vanessa J. Wong,
Tunbridge Wells, Kent, 1988

Peculiar Puritans

Especially in the late 16th and early 17th centuries, extreme Protestants known as Puritans chose names that expressed some virtue or religious slogan. They started out in England, especially in the counties of Kent, Sussex and Northamptonshire, but some travelled to America – the 'Pilgrim Fathers' who sailed to America in the ship Mayflower in 1620 and founded a colony were Puritans. There they continued to give babies these names. Although many of the names gradually died out, some, such as Faith, Hope, Charity, Felicity, Joy and Prudence, are still used.

● ●

Nicholas If-Jesus-Christ-Had-Not-Died-For-Thee-Thou-Hadst-Been-Damned Barebon

Born London c.1640; died Osterley, Middlesex, 1698
Son of Praise-God Barbon (after whom the 'Barebones Parliament' was named) and, following the Great Fire of London in 1666, inventor of fire insurance. He used the name Nicholas Barbon.

Magnify Beard

Baptized Warbleton, Sussex, 17 September 1587

Lament Bible

Married Nicholas Hussher, Ticehurst, Sussex, 9 September 1640

Mercye Bike
Baptized Thornhill by Dewsbury, Yorkshire, 9 February 1651

Fear Brewster
Born Scrooby, Nottinghamshire, *c*.1586
Fear, Patience, Love and Wrestling were among the Pilgrim Fathers who were aboard the Mayflower.

Repent Champney
Baptized Warbleton, Sussex, 14 August 1608

Clemency Chawncey
Buried St Dionis Backchurch, London, 27 August 1625

Be-Courteous Cole
Born Pevensey, Sussex, 1570

Changed Collins
(Female) Born Brightling, Sussex, 1 January 1598
She was the sister of:
Increased Collins
Born Brightling, Sussex, 30 March 1604

Redeemed Compton
Born Battle, Sussex, 1588

Diligence Constant
Buried St Peter upon Cornhill, London, 1 November 1724

God-help Cooper
Baptized Weybridge, Surrey, 12 June 1628

Sorry-for-sin Coupard
Baptized Warbleton, Sussex, 25 January 1589

Abuse-not Ellis
Baptized Warbleton, Sussex, 17 September 1592

Preserved Emms
(Female) Died St Nicholas', Yarmouth, 17 November 1712

More-fruit Fenner
Baptized Cranbrook, Kent, 22 December 1583
Dudley Fenner (c.1558–87), a Puritan preacher in Romford,
Essex, was accused of baptizing children with peculiar names
like Joy-again and From-above, but he explained that he had
given the same sort of names to his own children, including
More-fruit, Faint-not and Dust.

Replenish French
Baptized Warbleton, Sussex, 13 May 1660

Accepted Frewen
Baptized Northiam, Sussex, 26 May 1588;
died 28 March 1664
Accepted Frewen, brother of Thankfull Frewen
(born Northiam, Sussex, 1591; died 1656),
became Archbishop of York.

Joy-in-sorrow Godman
Married Joseph Baysie, All Saints',
Lewes, Sussex, 20 May 1614

Perseverance Green
(Female) Born Amsterdam, Netherlands, *c.*1603; arrived
Charlestown, Massachusetts, America, 1632

Hate-evil Greenhill
Baptized Banbury, Oxfordshire, 15 April 1660

Sin-deny Hely
(Female) Married William Swane,
Burwash, Sussex, 4 September 1621

Humiliation Hinde
Married Elizabeth Phillips, St Peter upon Cornhill,
London, 24 January 1629

Safe-on-high Hopkinson
Baptized Salehurst, Sussex, 28 February 1591

Opportunity Hopper
Married Thomas Lunt, Salem,
Massachusetts, America, 22 December 1680

Job-rakt-out-of-the-asshes [sic]
(Foundling) Baptized St Helen's, Bishopsgate,
London, 1 September 1611

First-borne and Sadness Luffe
(Female twins) Baptized Aylesbury,
Buckinghamshire, 2 September 1656

Free-gift and Fear-not Lulham
(Male twins) Baptized Warbleton, Sussex, 12 October 1589

Increase Mather
Born Dorchester, Massachusetts, America, 21 June 1629;
died Boston, Massachusetts, 23 August 1723
*Increase Mather was a Puritan clergyman, best known
for his involvement in the trials of people claimed to
be witches in Salem, Massachusetts, in 1692, which
resulted in 19 of them being hanged.*

Silence and Submit Meigs

Silence born Guilford, Connecticut, America, 5 January 1711;
Submit born Guilford 5 January 1712

Aydonhigh Mutlow

(Male) Baptized Bosbury, Herefordshire, 22 November 1601
*Aydonhigh (to be said as 'Aid On High') was the brother of
Comfort and Truth Mutlow.*

Hate Evil Nutter

Born England 1603; died Dover,
New Hampshire, America, 28 June 1675

Abstinence Pougher

(Male) Baptized St Nicholas, Leicester, 30 June 1672

Peaceable Sherwood

Baptized Thurlaston, Leicestershire, 15 January 1597
*He emigrated to America, and was recorded
as living in Virginia in 1623.*

Comfort Starr

Born Ashford, Kentucky, America, 11 April 1624;
died 30 October 1711

More-fruit Stone

(Male) Baptized Alfriston, Sussex, 6 June 1587
More-fruit was the father of:

Zealous Stone

(Male) Baptized Hellingley, Sussex, 8 March 1612

No-merit Vynall

(Female) Baptized Warbleton, Sussex, 28 September 1589

Continent Walker

(Female) Baptized Alfriston, Sussex, 22 December 1594

Discretion Watkinson
Married Elizabeth Wild, South Muskham,
Nottinghamshire, 17 November 1659

Restored Weekes
Married Constant Sumar, Chiddingly, Sussex, 27 August 1618

Faint-not Wood
Married William Clarke, Laughton, Sussex, 24 December 1618

Repentance Wrath
(Male) Baptized Elham, Kent, 26 March 1612

Rejoice Wratten
(Female) Baptized Warbleton, Sussex, 18 October 1679

Name Games

*Some of the names that follow are a little
different from the more 'accidental' names in the
rest of the book in that they were deliberate –
parents gave their children very long, rhyming
or other unusual names to make them stand out.*

LONG AND LOONY

**Luquincy Raine Martha Jane Eldorado
Julie Dean Delma Ruthie Matilda
Felma Jacka Cina Sophi Husky
Charlotte Moss Stone Banks**

Born Alabama c.1855 (Walker, Alabama, 1880 US census)
*Known to her family and friends as Lu-Ma, she died aged 100
in Jasper, Alabama.*

Autumn Sullivan Corbett Fitzsimmons Jeffries Hart Burns Johnson Willard Dempsey Tunney Schmeling Sharkey Carnera Baer Braddock Louis Charles Walcott Marciano Patterson Johansson Liston Clay Frazier Foreman Brown

Born Wolverhampton 2007

Autumn received the names of boxing champions. Her mother, Maria, also had many names, as did her aunt Rebecca (34 names) and uncle Brian (42 names of bare-knuckle fighters).

Xenophilus Epaphreditus Baycock Calvert

Died Huddersfield, Yorkshire, 1842

Zaphnathpaaneah Isaiah Obededom Nicodemus Francis Edward Clarke

Baptized Beccles, Suffolk, 14 October 1804

Only Francis Edward would fit in the parish register, so the other names had to be added at the bottom.

La Rhennee Le Veghonora Jannette Betsey Restall De Louth

Born Midhurst, Hampshire, 1850

Tee-Goo-Gee-Tah Te-Ha-Le-To-Hih Te-Coo-Gee-Tah Dumpling

Born Cherokee Nation, Dakota, USA, 1827

**Louis George Maurice Adolph Roch
Albert Abel Antonio Alexandre
Noë Jean Lucien Daniel Eugène
Joseph-le-brun Joseph-Barême Thomas
Thomas Thomas-Thomas Pierre
Arbon Pierre-Maurel Barthélemi
Artus Alphonse Bertrand Dieudonné
Emanuel Josué Vincent Luc Michel
Jules-de-la-Plane Jules-Bazin
Julio César Jullien**

Born Sisteron, France, 23 April 1812; died Neuilly-sur-Seine,
France, 14 March 1860

*He was a French conductor and composer whose
parents were persuaded by the 36 members of the Sisteron
Philharmonic Society that they should all be godfathers,
and who received all their names. He was usually known
simply as 'The Maestro' (the Master).*

**Edith Kekuhikuhikuhipuuoneonaaliio-
kohala Kanaele Kanakaole**

Born 30 October 1913; died Hilo,
Hawaii, USA, October 1979

She was an expert on Hawaiian culture and hula dancing.

**Xenia Marelina Veronique
Caroline Sophia Murray Moore**

Born Richmond, Surrey, 1888

**Thomas Hill Joseph Napoleon Horatio
Bonaparte Swindlehurst Nelson**

Born Preston, Lancashire, 1839

Tracy Mariclaire Lisa Tammy Samantha
Christine Alexandra Candy Bonnie Ursula
Zoe Nichola Patricia Lynda Kate Jean
Sandra Karren Julie Jane Elizabeth
Felicity Gabriella Jackie Corina
Constance Arabella Clara Honor
Geraldine Giona Erika Fillippa Anabel
Elsie Amanda Cheryl Alanna Louise Angie
Beth Crystal Dawn Debbie Eileen Grace
Susan Rebecca Valerie Kay Lena
Margaret Anna Amy Carol Bella Avril Ava
Audry Andrea Daphne Donna Cynthia
Cassie Christable Vivien Wendy Moira
Jennifer Abbie Adelaide Carissa Clara
Anne Astrid Barbara Clarissa Catalina
Bonny Dee Hazel Iris Anthea Clarinda
Bernadette Cara Alison Carrie Angela
Beryl Caroline Emma Dana Vanessa Zara
Violet Lynn Maggie Pamela Rosemary
Ruth Cathlene Alexandrina Annette
Hilary Diana Angelina Carrinna Victoria
Sara Mandy Annabella Beverley Bridget
Cecilia Catherine Brenda Jessica Isabella
Delilah Camila Candice Helen Connie
Charmaine Dorothy Melinda Nancy Marian
Vicki Selina Miriam Norma Pauline Toni
Penny Shari Zsa Zsa Queenie Nelson

Born Chesterfield, Derbyshire, 31 December 1985

Maria de los Dolores Petrona Ramona Juana Nepomucena Josefa Cayetana Beatriz de la Santisima Trinidad North

Born c.1811; died Lambeth, London, 1890

Ann Bertha Cecilia Diana Emily Fanny Gertrude Hypatia Inez Jane Kate Louisa Maud Nora Ophelia Quince Rebecca Starkey Teresa Ulysis Venus Winifred Xenophen Yetty Zeus Pepper

Born West Derby, Lancashire, 19 December 1882
She was given a name for each letter of the alphabet, except that of her surname, in alphabetical order.

The Honourable Sir Reginald Aylmer Ranfurly Plunkett-Ernle-Erle-Drax

Born London 28 August 1880; died Poole, Dorset, 16 October 1967

Charles Caractacus Ostorius Maximillian Gustavus Adolphus Stone

Baptized Burbage, Wiltshire, 29 April 1781

Richard Plantagenet Campbell Temple-Nugent-Brydges-Chandos-Grenville

Born 10 September 1823; died London 26 March 1882
He was the 3rd Duke and 4th Marquis of Buckingham.

The Tollemache Family

The Reverend Ralph William Lyonel Tollemache (1826–95) was a clergyman in South Wytham, near Grantham, Lincolnshire. With his first wife, his cousin Caroline Tollemache (1828–67), he had five children to whom he gave the names:

Lyonel Felix Carteret Eugene Tollemache

(1854–1952)

Florence Caroline Artemisia Hume Tollemache

(1855–1935)

Evelyne Clementina Wentworth Cornelia Maude Tollemache

(1856–1919)

Granville Gray Marchmont Manners Plantagenet Tollemache

(1858–91)

Marchmont Murray Reginald Grasett Stanhope Plantagenet Tollemache

(1860–98)

After the death of his first wife, in 1869 he married Dora Cleopatra Maria Lorenza de Orellana y Revest (c.1847–1929) and gave their ten children even longer names:

Dora Viola Gertrude Irenez de Orellana Dysart Plantagenet Tollemache-Tollemache

(1869–74)

Mabel Helmingham Ethel Huntingtower Beatrice Blazonberrie Evangeline Vise de Lou de Orellana Plantagenet Saxon Toedmag Tollemache-Tollemache

(1872–1955)

Lyonesse Matilda Dora Ida Agne Ernestine Curson Paulet Wilbraham Joyce Eugénie Bentley Saxonia Dysart Plantagenet Tollemache-Tollemache

(1874-1944)

Lyulph Ydwallo Odin Nestor Egbert Lyonel Toedmag Hugh Erchenwyne Saxon Esa Cromwell Orma Nevill Dysart Plantagenet Tollemache-Tollemache

(1876-1961)

The initial letters of his first names spell 'Lyonel the Second'.

Lyona Decima Veronica Esyth Undine Cyssa Hylda Rowena Viola Adela Thyra Ursula Ysabel Blanche Lelias Dysart Plantagenet Tollemache-Tollemache

(1878-1962)

Leo Quintus Tollemache-Tollemache de Orellana Plantagenet Tollemache-Tollemache

(1879–1914)

In 1908 he gave up all but the first and last of his names.

Lyonella Fredegunda Cuthberga Ethelswytha Ideth Ysabel Grace Monica de Orellana Plantagenet Tollemache-Tollemache

(1882–1952)

Leone Sextus Denys Oswolf Fraudatifilius Tollemache-Tollemache de Orellana Plantagenet Tollemache-Tollemache

(1884–1917)

Lyonetta Edith Regina Valentine Myra Polwarth Avelina Philippa Violantha de Orellana Plantagenet Tollemache-Tollemache

(1887–1951)

Lynonulph Cospatrick Bruce Berkeley Jermyn Tullibardine Petersham de Orellana Dysart Plantagenet Tollemache-Tollemache

(1892–1966)

Henry Edward Montague Dorington Clotworthy Upton

Born Kensington, London, 1853

Dancell Dallphebo Marc Antony Dallery Gallery Caesar Williams

Baptized Old Swinford, Worcestershire, 28 January 1676

He was the son of another Dancell Dallphebo Marc Antony Dallery Gallery Caesar Williams.

Louis George Maurice Adolphe Roche Albert Abel Antonio Alexandre Noë Jean Lucien Daniel Eugène Joseph-le-brun Joseph-Barême Thomas Rhoshandiatellyneshiaunneveshenk Koyaanfsquatsiuty Williams

Born Beaumont, Texas, USA, 12 September 1984

The son of James L. Williams and Cosandra Lloydette Ward, he later expanded his name to 1,019 letters.

Adolph Blaine Charles David Earl Frederick Gerald Hubert Irvin John Kenneth Lloyd Martin Nero Oliver Paul Quincy Randolph Sherman Thomas Uncas Victor William Xerxes Yancy Wolfeschlegelsteinhausen-bergerdorffwelchevoralternwar engewissenschaftschaferswes-senschafewarenwohlg epflegeund-sorgfaltigkeitbeschutzenvonangreif eudurchihrraubgierigfeindewelchev-oralternzwolftausendjahresvorandieer-scheinenerscheinenvan derersteerde-menschderraumschiffgebrauchlichta Isseinu rsprungv onkraftg est art-seinlangefahrthinzwischensternaiti-graumaufdersuchenachdiesternwelc hegehabt bewohnbarplanetenk-reisedrehensichundwohinderne-

**urassevonverstandigmenschlich-
keitkonntefortpflanzenundsicher-
feuenanlebenslanglichfreudeun-
druhemitnicheinfurchtvorangreifenvo-
nandererintelligentgeschopfsvonhinz-
wischenternartigraum Senior**

*Born near Hamburg on Leap Year day, 29 February 1904, he
is said to have emigrated to the United States and lived in
Philadelphia, where he became known as Wolfe+585. He is
claimed to have shortened his name to Wolfeschlegelstein-
hausenbergerdorff, and was also known as Hubert Blaine
Wolfe. However, despite appearing in* Guinness World Records
*and other respected reference works, and on many websites,
there appears to be no official record of his existence, and it
seems possible that his remarkable name was a hoax.*

SHORT AND SWEET
• • • • • • • • • • • • • •

**There are quite a lot of people with single-letter first
names and surnames, but they are often confused with
initials. In May 1996 A (said to be pronounced 'Albin')
was the name given to a Swedish child after the first
name Brfxxccxxmnpccccclllmmnprxvclmnckssqlbb11116
was officially rejected – but this name was also
rejected. Here are some examples of the many
people with two-letter surnames.**

Gertrude Aa
Born 16 January 1929; died Maui,
Hawaii, USA, 15 November 2005

Manuela Bonaventura Ab
Born Lima, Peru, 22 March 1818

Susannah Ad

Baptized St Andrew's, Enfield, Middlesex, 5 December 1753

Tip Ah

Married Hi Toy, Calaveras, California, USA, 4 March 1862

Anne Ax

Married Joseph Barrowclough, Kirkburton, Yorkshire, 1 October 1728

Bessie Bo

Born Hawick, Roxburgh, 17 December 1650

Bob By

Born Battle, Sussex, c.1841 (Battle, 1841 England census)

Ed Ek

Born 22 January 1877; died International Falls, Minnesota, USA, August 1972

Ebenezer Ha

Married Agens Orr, Likmaurs, Ayrshire, 19 October 1839

Ze Oh

Born 1 September 1895; died South Bend, Indiana, April 1979

An Ox

Baptized Lowestoft, Suffolk, 12 May 1611

Septimus Py

Born Out Rawcliffe, Lancashire, c.1847
(Out Rawcliffe, 1851 England census)

Robert Re

Married Jone [sic] Streat, St Gregory's, Dawlish, Devon, 6 January 1647

Abraham Sy
Born Thorney, Cambridge, 3 March 1667

Te Ta
Born 1 July 1898; died San Jose,
California, USA, 2 January 1985

John Wo
Born Leasingham, Lincolnshire, 30 July 1771

Emily Yo
Baptized Sutton-Benger, Wiltshire, 15 March 1839

RHYME TIME
● ● ● ● ● ● ● ● ● ● ●

Mabel Abel
Born Norwich, Norfolk, c.1895
(Norwich, 1901 England census)

Sally Alley
Born Yorkshire c.1825
(Halifax, Yorkshire, 1841 England census)

R. V. Arvey
Born 24 October 1897 (Chicago,
Illinois, USA, First World War draft registration)

Hayley Bailey
Born Southend, Essex, 1977

Paul Ball
Baptized Bath Abbey, Somerset, 7 February 1599

Charley Barley
Born New Cross, Kent, c.1857
(Croydon, Surrey, 1861 England census)

Neamon Beamon
Born 15 April 1909; died Chicago, Illinois, USA, 15 April 1991

Phoebe Beebe
Born Michigan c.1857 (Pulaski, Michigan, 1860 US census)

Sibyl Bibble
Born Barking, Suffolk, c.1637; married Myles Nutt 2 July 1671

Blanch Branch
Born Rhode Island c.1877
(Providence, Rhode Island, 1930 US census)

Fred Bread
Born c.1818; died Halifax, Yorkshire, 1875

Lizzie Busy
Baptized Modbury, Devon, 18 July 1632

Harry Carry
Born Folkestone, Kent, c.1868
(Folkestone, 1901 England census)

Ace Case
Born Wisconsin c.1852 (Westport,
Wisconsin, 1860 US census)

Terry Cherry
(Female) Born Illinois c.1835 (Cheney Grove,
Illinois, 1850 US census)

Hester Chester
Born Blackburn, Lancashire, 1862

Nancy Clancy
Born Brent, Devon, *c*.1847 (Brent, 1871 England census)

Beverley Cleveley
Married Stephen Reynolds, Solihull, West Midlands, 2000

Box Cox
(Female) Born Iowa *c*.1887 (Chicago, Illinois, 1920 US census)

Jack Crack
Born Bury St Edmunds, Suffolk, 1909

Shirley Curley
Born 1940; died Greenwich, London, 2002

Mary Dairy
Married John Homes, Whitgift, Yorkshire, 10 January 1809

Nancy Dancy
Born North Carolina *c*.1812 (Mulberry,
North Carolina, 1870 US census)

Andy Dandy
Baptized St Stephen Walbrook, London, 28 May 1712

Mark Dark
Born Keynsham, Somerset, 1867

Sybil Dibble
Born New York *c*.1845 (Stephentown,
New York, 1850 US census)

Vito Dincognito
Born Illinois 2 June 1917; died Los Angeles,
California, USA, 21 June 1971

Heather Feather
Married Peter McClelland, Keighley, Yorkshire, 1992

Trish Fish
Born South Dakota c.1918 (Hennepin,
Minnesota, 1920 US census)

Guy Fly
Born Tennessee c.1802 (Blaine, Washington, 1910 US census)

Wong Bong Fong
Born China c.1884; died York, Ontario, Canada, 3 June 1927

Sandy Gandy
(Male) Born Alabama c.1844 (Lavaca, Texas, 1870 US census)

Hugh Glue
Married Ann White, Chelsea, London, 1804

Norman Gorman
Born Pendleton, Lancashire, c.1884
(Pendleton, 1891 England census)

Mary Hairy
Married Helmsley, Yorkshire, 1861

Paris Harris
Born Illinois c.1856 (Green, Missouri, 1870 US census)

Fred Head
Born Stockbridge, Hampshire, 1865

Milton Hilton
Born California c.1898 (Santa Barbara,
California, 1910 US census)

Newton Hooton
Born 15 June 1920; passenger on *Westernland*, Antwerp,
Belgium–New York, USA, arrived 17 August 1937

Rose Hose
Born Retford, Nottinghamshire, 1871
(Laneham, Nottinghamshire, 1871 England census)

Nelly Jelly
Born Croydon, London, 1892

Polly Jolly
Born West Ham, Essex, 1921

Sidney Kidney
Born Milton, Kent, 1906

Peg Legg
Born Stuntney, Cambridgeshire, c.1900
(Ely, Cambridgeshire, 1901 England census)

Mink Link
(Male) Born Germany 1837 (Danton,
North Dakota, 1900 US census)

Casey Macy
Born Los Angeles, California, USA, 12 March 1981

Stacy Macy
Born Indiana c.1873 (Posey, Indiana, 1880 US census)

Channing Manning
Born 22 June 1907; died Santa Cruz,
California, USA, 5 July 1969

Zaiboon McDoom
Born 11 November 1916; died Waltham Forest, London, 2003

Trudy Moody
Married Robert Eaton, Southampton, Hampshire, 1990

June Moon
Born Bedfordshire c.1801 (Bedford, 1841 England census)

Hatty Patty
Born Chelsea, London, c.1830
(Islington, London, 1851 England census)

Kenny Penny
Born c.1887 (Beecher, Wisconsin, 1930 US census)

Berry Perry
Born 16 July 1888; died Oakwood,
Texas, USA, 15 January 1975

Mary Scary
Born Docking, Norfolk, 1843

Goon Soon
Born 12 March 1897; died Boston,
Massachusetts, USA, 20 October 1981

Frank Stank
Born 29 November 1893; died Taylor Springs,
Illinois, USA, December 1968

Liquid Cate Tate
Born Alamance, North Carolina, USA, 1930

Fang Wang
Married Chardphong Phobkoonthod,
Plymouth, Devon, July 2005

Max Wax
Married St Giles', London, 1911

Goodman Woodman
Married Hailsham, Sussex, 1699

MUDDLED MONIKERS
*The letters of the first and second names are the same,
but in a different order.*
● ● ● ● ● ● ● ● ● ● ● ● ● ● ● ● ●

Abel Able
(Male) Born Vanderburgh, Indiana, USA, 1 July 1893

Mary Army
Married Aron [*sic*] Memory, St Andrew's,
Plymouth, Devon, 6 October 1663

Ronald Arnold
Born Bedford 1885

Abel Bale
Born Market Harborough, Leicestershire, 1844

Albert Bartel
Born Battersea, London, c.1889
(Lambeth, London, 1891 England census)

Bertha Bather
Born Peover, Cheshire, c.1880
(Chelford, Cheshire, 1901 England census)

Brian Brain
Born 1942; died Worcester 1997

Nancy Canny
Married Stephen Hoit, Athens, Ohio, USA, 25 December 1823

Clare Clear
Born Stepney, London, 1896

Lydia Daily
Baptized St John de Sepulchre,
Norwich, Norfolk, 25 May 1748

Dale Deal
Born 28 November 1935; died Titusville,
Pennsylvania, USA, July 1983

Edna Dean
Baptized Stalybridge, Cheshire, 5 November 1797

Denis Dines
Born 1923; died Tower Hamlets, London, 1991

Leo Elo
Born Massachusetts c.1916 (Worcester,
Massachusetts, 1920 US census)

Gary Gray
Born South Carolina *c.*1901 (Greenville,
South Carolina, 1920 US census)

Thelma Hamlet
Born Aston, Warwickshire, 1909

Ruth Hurt
Baptized Alfreton, Derbyshire, 29 August 1731

Jane Jean
Baptized Stoke Climsland, Cornwall, 7 February 1830

Neal Lane
Born 24 October 1919; died Fayetteville,
North Carolina, USA, 12 September 1998

Charles Larches
Born Bethnal Green, London, *c.*1890
(Bethnal Green, 1891 England census)

Mildred Middler
Born 30 October 1910; died Detroit,
Michigan, USA, 27 July 1981

Romeo Moore
Born 28 December 1898; died Victor,
West Virginia, USA, 1 March 1988

Norma Moran
Born 20 December 1897; died Los Angeles,
California, USA, 7 September 1971

Ann Nan
Born Bradford, Yorkshire, 1868

Ernest Nester
Born West Ham, Essex, 1895

Mary Ramy
Born Stepney, London, c.1838
(Willesden, London, 1871 England census)

Vera Rave
Born 10 August 1905; died La Salle,
Illinois, USA, November 1980

Earl Real
Born 27 February 1905; died Chicago,
Illinois, USA, 5 April 1975

Eric Rice
Born Bromley, Kent, 1901

Eros Rose
Born Amesbury, Wiltshire, 1884

Rosa Soar
Born Ticknall, Derbyshire, c.1858
(Ticknall, 1861 England census)

Rose Sore
Born Stowmarket, Suffolk, c.1867
(Bradford, Yorkshire, 1901 England census)

Andrew Wander
Married Jane Little, Wamphray, Dumfries, 19 July 1835

Lewis Wiles
Born 21 May 1839; baptized St Peter Mancroft,
Norwich, Norfolk, 25 September 1839

BACK TO FRONT

Palindromes – sentences, words or, in this case, names – spelled the same backwards as forwards. With some, just the first or second name is a palindrome, for example:

• • • • • • • • • • • • •

Asa Reynolds

Born Nine Partners, New York, 1759; died Granville, New York, USA, 25 December 1834

On 24 October 1782 Asa Reynolds married Hannah Wells in Dutchess County, New York. Both had first names that were palindromes and named all their 12 children in the same way: Hannah, Asa, Emme, Iri, Aziza, Anna, Zerez, Axa, Atta, Alila, Numun and Harrah. In 1834 Harrah married a woman called Hannah and had a son called Asa, hence completing a run of palindromes – Asa–Hannah–Harrah–Hannah–Asa – that was itself a palindrome.

There are some names where both the first and second names are palindromes, such as:

Hannah Tippit

Baptized Sheffield Cathedral, 12 March 1756

And there are others where the whole name is a palindrome – try these out:

Abba Abba

Born Leicestershire 1987

Elba Able

(Female) Born Texas 1881 (Concho, Texas, 1900 US census)
Her name reminds us that the Emperor Napoleon, who was imprisoned on the island of Elba, is claimed to have said: 'Able was I ere I saw Elba' – the whole sentence is a palindrome.

Ada Ada
Born Stone, Staffordshire, c.1855
(Longton, Staffordshire, 1901 England census)

Nell Allen
Born Leeds, Yorkshire, 1884

Anna Anna
Born Bradford, Yorkshire, c.1850
(Birkenhead, Cheshire, 1851 England census)

Mary Byram
Baptized Deane by Bolton, Lancashire, 16 September 1629

Anna Danna
Born 7 February 1921; died Abita Springs,
Louisiana, USA, 7 March 2008

Anna D'Anna
Born 1925; died Aylesbury, Buckinghamshire, 2001

Enid Dine
Born Edmonton, Middlesex, 1900
Her mother Ada also had a palindromic first name.

Elle G. Elle
Born Dover, Kent, c.1900 (Dover, 1901 England census)

Eve Eve
Born Essex c.1828 (High Easter, Essex, 1841 England census)

Hannah Hannah
Born Erpingham, Norfolk, 1846

Norabel LeBaron
Born Michigan c.1907 (Tork, Michigan, 1910 US census)

Noel Leon

Married Julia Stevens, Salisbury, Wiltshire, 2003

Neil Lien

Born 18 August 1883; died Wisconsin, USA, 14 March 1964

Tom Mot

Born 1906; died Colchester, Essex, 1990

Revilo Oliver

Born Beaminster, Dorset, 1851

Ono Ono

Born Kuinolei, Honolulu, Hawaii, c.1853

Otto Otto

Born Berne, Switzerland, c.1879
(St Pancras, London, 1901 England census)

Yendis Sidney

Born West Ham, Essex, 1900

Robert Trebor

Born France c.1879; passenger on *Normandie*, Le Havre,
France–New York, USA, arrived 12 April 1937

21

The Name's the Same . . .

HILARIOUS HISTORY

Boadicea Basher

Baptized St Hilary, Cornwall, 13 January 1856
*Boadicea (also spelled Boudicca) was the first-century AD
queen of the Iceni tribe who fought against the Romans.*

Napoleon Bonaparte

Born 12 November 1892; died Steele,
Minnesota, USA, 19 February 1982

*The more famous Napoleon Bonaparte was the French
Emperor at the beginning of the 19th century.*

Emily Pocohontas [*sic*] Brown

Born Gravesend, Kent, 1847

Although best known from the 1995 Disney film, Pocahontas,
*after whom – though with a slightly different spelling –
Emily Pocohontas Brown was named, was a Native American
princess who was brought to England in 1616 and died of
smallpox the following year. She was buried in the graveyard of
St George's church, Gravesend, which may be why the name
was chosen as a middle name for Emily Brown, who lived
there and may even have been baptized in St George's.*

Julius Caesar

Married Alice Dente, Mitcham, Surrey, 10 April 1596

Winston Churchill

Born Missouri c.1872 (St Louis, Missouri, 1880 US census)

*This Winston Churchill was born in the USA two years
before the famous British politician and Second World
War leader Winston Churchill.*

Christopher Columbus

Born 28 November 1928; died Columbia, South Carolina,
USA, 15 March 2009

*This modern Christopher Columbus lived in
Columbia, a city named after the explorer.*

William Conqueror

Born Sunderland, Durham, 1862

Captain Cook

Born Bury, Lancashire, 1850

'Captain' was his first name; he was named after the famous explorer Captain (James) Cook (1728–79).

William The Second Davy

Born Romford, Essex, 1890

'William The Second' were his first three names.

Albert Einstein

Born Munich, Germany, 30 December 1880;
died 13 February 1952

Not the Albert Einstein, this one was born a year after the famous scientist, but also in Germany, and died three years before him.

Guy Fawkes

Born Louisiana c.1810 (Rosa Bar, California, 1860 US census)

As Guy Fawkes, one of the 1605 Gunpowder Plot conspirators, was regarded as a villain, few people have ever received the same name.

Princess Diana Frempong

Born Wandsworth, London, 2004

King George

Baptized St Martin-in-the-Fields, London, 27 May 1724

'King' was his first name – King George I was on the throne at the time of his birth.

The Six Wives of Henry VIII

• • • • • • • • • • • • • • • • • • • •

Catherine Aragon

Born Ireland c.1870 (Manhattan, New York, 1930 US census)

Anne Boleyn

Born Cork, Ireland, c.1850
(Soho, London, 1881 England census)
This royal namesake was an Irish dressmaker living in London.

Jane Seymour

Born Pontefract, Yorkshire, 1909
*This Jane Seymour was born 400 years after Henry VIII's
third wife, but there were more than 800 Jane Seymours
born in the period 1837–2005.*

Anne Cleves

Baptized Toot Baldon, Oxfordshire, 22 February 1735

Catherine Howard

Born 1 August 1882; died Morristown, New Jersey, USA,
March 1974

Catherine Parr

Born Eccleston, Lancashire, 1 May 1677

———————————

Abraham and Joe Hitler

(Twins) Born Prestwich, Lancashire, 1901
*Being called Hitler in 1901 was not a problem, but by
the Second World War 'Hitler' had become one of
the most hated names in the world.*

Martin Luther King

Born Texas c.1878 (Nacogdoches, Texas, 1880 US census)
*This Martin Luther King was born more than 50 years
before the famous civil rights leader.*

Abraham Lincoln

Baptized Octagon Chapel, Norwich, Norfolk, 6 June 1720
*This baby, whose father was also called Abraham Lincoln,
was born nearly 90 years before the Abraham Lincoln
who became US President.*

Horatio Nelson

Born Beccles, Suffolk, 28 July 1751; died November 1751
*This Horatio Nelson was born and died seven years before the
great British admiral was born in the next county of Norfolk.
Following his naval victories in the Napoleonic Wars and his
heroic death at the Battle of Trafalgar in 1815, hundreds of
Nelson boys were given the first name 'Horatio'.*

Florence Nightingale

Born Chesterfield, Derbyshire, 1855
*After the famous nurse Florence Nightingale became famous
during the Crimean War, almost 1,000 female Nightingale
babies were named after her.*

Pocahontas Pharaoh

Born 15 February 1878; died New York, USA, January 1963

William Shakespeare

Died Wroxall, Warwickshire, 14 April 1551
*This William Shakespeare, the son of Richard Shakespeare
and Alice Griffin, lived in the same county as the famous
playwright, but died 13 years before he was born.*

Shake Spear

Born Georgia c.1885 (Cane Creek, Georgia, 1930 US census)

Queen Victoria

Born c.1840 (Edmonton, Middlesex, 1851 England census)
'Queen' was her first name.

General Washington

Born Halifax, Yorkshire, 1842
'General' was his first name, but he was probably named after American General George Washington, the first US President.

Lady Godiva A. Wright

Born Brixton, Devon, c.1849
(Plymouth, Devon, 1891 England census)
'Lady Godiva' were her first names. She was named after the 11th-century noblewoman who, according to legend, rode naked through the streets of Coventry to make her husband Leofric relieve the local peasants of taxation.

Some parents have given their children names that commemorate important historical events, such as battles.

Ypres Bushby

Born Guisborough, Yorkshire, 1914
Before the First World War battles of Ypres in 1914 and 1915, almost no one was called 'Ypres', but during the war, more than 50 British babies received it as a first name, perhaps to commemorate a father or other family member who had died.

John Lucknow Hidden Carpenter

Born Upton-upon-Severn, Worcestershire, 1859
His name probably commemorated the Siege of Lucknow, India, two years earlier.

Norman Conquest

Born Lewisham, London, 1904

Agincourt Charles Crispin

Born Ampthill, Bedfordshire, 1855

The Battle of Agincourt was fought on St Crispin's Day
(25 October) 1415, so Agincourt's parents must have
thought it would be a good idea to name him after it.

Godfrey Armistice Day

Born 11 November 1923; died Milton Keynes,
Buckinghamshire, 2003

The date of his birth, 11 November 1923, was the fifth
anniversary of Armistice Day, the day when the fighting
of the First World War ended.

Abraham Lincoln Death

Born Epping, Essex, 1876

US President Abraham Lincoln had been assassinated in 1865.

Jane Trafalgar Grapes

Born Newport, Isle of Wight, 1805

Jane was one of the children of John and Hannah Grapes, who
were all given middle names relating to the Napoleonic Wars.
They included Charles Wellington Grapes (1811), named after
British general the Duke of Wellington, while Jane, William Nile
Grapes (1815) and Charlotte Waterloo Grapes (1815) were
named after important battles.

Centennial Ham

Born 15 April 1876; died Markleville, Indiana, USA, May 1969

The 1876 Centennial was a commemoration of the 100th
anniversary of the creation of the United States. In that year,
many children were given 'Centennial' as a first name.

Pearl Harbor Johnson

Born Granville, North Carolina, USA, 24 March 1943
*The Japanese attack on the US Navy base at Pearl Harbor,
Hawaii, on 7 December 1941 was the event that brought the
United States into the Second World War.*

Mabel Jubi Lee

Born Peterborough, Northamptonshire, 1897
*Mabel was named as a tribute to Queen Victoria, who
celebrated her Diamond Jubilee – the 60th year
of her reign – in this year.*

Edwin Titanic Pascoe

Born 1912; died Penzance, Cornwall, 1996
He was born twelve days before the Titanic *disaster,
but perhaps named to commemorate its launch.*

William Waterloo Napoleon Saunders

Born Sutton Courtney, Berkshire, *c.*1868
(Brighton, Sussex, 1881 England census)
*William Waterloo Napoleon Saunders was named after the
British defeat of Napoleon and the French army at the
Battle of Waterloo in 1815. He was the elder brother
of Pius Romulus Saunders.*

BIBLICAL NAMES

● ● ● ● ● ● ● ● ● ● ● ●

Cain Abel

Born 27 July 1751, Norwich, Norfolk

Eve Adam

Born 8 January 1880; died Nome,
Alaska, USA, 15 October 1968

John Baptist
Baptized St Lawrence Pountney, London, 11 September 1543

David Goliath Bayliss
Born Guildford, Surrey, 1880
*Named after the biblical story of David and Goliath,
fishmonger David Goliath Bayliss gave all his children strange
names, including giving one his own middle name, Goliath
(born 1914), as well as Strange Conveyance Victory (1916),
Vengeance Recompense Faith (1919), Wholesome
Dwell (1920) and Dorothy Newdwell (1922).*

Judas Iscariot Burton
Born Stafford 1882

Adam Eve
Baptized Little Dunmow, Essex, 26 October 1624

Shadrach Meshach Abednego
Daniel Goldsmith
Born Stow, Suffolk, 1849

Mary Magdalene
Married Henry Blackmeere, St Mary Woolnoth,
London, 18 May 1630

Pontius Pilate
Born Alexandria, Louisiana, USA, 10 May 1877

Lot Salt
Baptized Wirksworth, Derbyshire, 15 December 1795

Delilah Samson
Born Hounslow, London, 2005

King Solomon
Baptized Bodiam, Sussex, 12 April 1835

Mahershalalhashbaz Sturgeon
Born Hessett, Suffolk, *c.*1857 (Hessett, 1881 England census)
Mahershalalhashbaz, the son of Isaiah, is the longest
personal name in the Bible.

Jonah Whalebelly
Born Saham Toney, Norfolk, *c.*1818
(Saham Toney, 1891 England census)

NURSERY NONSENSE

Butcher Baker
Born Texas c.1866 (Limestone, Texas, 1880 US census)

Baby Bunting
(Female) Born Matlock, Derbyshire, c.1900
(Matlock, 1901 England census)

King Cole
Born Wortley, Yorkshire, 1883

Mary Contrare
Born 17 November 1905; died Queens,
New York, USA, 16 October 1989

Marjorie Daw
Born Wandsworth, London, 1891

Thomas Dumpty
Died Liverpool, Lancashire, 1862

Kitty Fisher
Died St Saviour, Southwark, London, 1845

Polly Flinders
Born Caxton, Cambridgeshire, 1875

Alfred Doctor Foster
Died Preston, Lancashire, 1846

Solomon Grundy
Died Bolton, Lancashire, 1865

Jack Horner
Born West Derby, Lancashire, 1895

Lucy Lockett
Married Aston, Warwickshire, 1840

Miss Muffet
Unnamed female Muffet, born Swaffham, Norfolk, 1841

Henny Penny
(Male) Born Llanasa, Flintshire, c.1839
(Llanasa, 1901 Wales census)

Peter Piper
Baptized Lavenham, Suffolk, 8 April 1582

Jack B. Nimble
Divorced from Jane Nimble, Miami-Dade,
Florida, USA, 25 September 1992

George Porges
Born Manchester, Lancashire, c.1869
(Pendlebury and Swinton, Lancashire, 1901 England census)

Jack B. Quick
Born 19 March 1929; died Colorado Springs,
Colorado, USA, 15 February 2008

Cock Robin
Born c.1865 (Crayford, Kent, 1901 England census)

Anthony Rowley
Married Mary Dennis, Kingston upon Thames,
Surrey, 22 December 1706

Bobby Shafto
Born Liverpool, Lancashire, 1846

Simple Simon
Born Poland c.1865 (Nashville, Tennessee, 1930 US census)

Jack Spratt
Born Epsom, Surrey, 1906

Bopeep Story
(Male) Born c.1917 (Oxford, North Carolina, 1930 US census)

Sarah Tinker Taylor
Died Bolton, Lancashire, 1845

Tommy Tucker
Born Clutton, Somerset, 1838

Willie Winkie
Married Janet Logan, St Ninians, Stirling, 7 November 1784

Jenny Wren
Born Fulham, London, 1890

FANTASTIC FICTION

• • • • • • • • • • • • • • • • •

King Arthur

Born Lambeth, London, c.1863
(Fulham, London, 1901 England census)
The King Arthur after whom this baby was named was a
legendary king who appears in many stories, but
there is no real evidence that he existed.

Ali Baba

Born Prussia *c.*1868 (Venice, California, 1920 US census)

Cinderella Ball

Born Indiana *c.*1862 (Monroe, Indiana, 1880 US census)

Bruce Batman

Born 14 September 1942; died Interlachen,
Florida, USA, 26 June 2007
The comic book character Batman *(real name Bruce Wayne)*
first appeared in May 1939 Detective Comics *No. 27.*

Rupert Bear

Born Stratford, Essex, *c.*1878 (Harrow,
Middlesex, 1881 England census)

Three Bears

(Male) Born *c.*1851 (Montana, 1910 US Indian census)

Fabiola Thumbelina Blonigen

Born Hennepin, Minnesota, USA, 26 April 1935

King Arthur Bosworth

Born North Hampton, Massachusetts, 28 May 1887;
died Tiffin, Ohio, USA, 1 May 1953
*As well as his royal first names, this American had a
surname which is that of the battle at which British
king Richard III was killed in 1485.*

Bob Builder

Married Susanna Sproll, St Philip and St Jacob,
Bristol, Gloucestershire, 8 October 1778

Benjamin Bunny

Son of Abraham and Elizabeth Bunny, baptized Glenfield,
Leicestershire, 25 December 1749

Bambam Brendon Carmichael

Born Hale, Texas, USA, 17 January 1930

Robinson Crusoe

Born Devon *c*.1811 (Stoke Damerel,
Devon, 1841 England census)

Donald Duck

Born Edmonton, Middlesex, 1899
Donald Duck was the brother of Rhoda Duck.

Ernst Gollum

Born Germany c.1820 (Jefferson, Ohio, 1870 US census)

Hephzibah Gromit

Married Boston, Lincolnshire, 1855

Etheleen Prince Hamlet

Born 17 November 1949; died Wagener,
South Carolina, USA, 28 February 2008
*She was named after William Shakespeare's
most famous male character.*

Gulielinus Hobbit

(Male) Married Margaretam [*sic*] Rayer, Swindon,
Gloucestershire, 22 July 1607

James Riding Hood

Married Clifton, Gloucestershire, 1875

Robin Hood

Married Alice Sherwood, Farndon,
Nottinghamshire, 4 June 1707

Indiana Jones

Born 13 May 1897; died Chicago, Illinois, USA, 11 May 1971

Jedi Key-Ras-Tafari S. Knight

Born Birmingham, Warwickshire, 1998

Stuart Little

Born Newcastle upon Tyne, Northumberland, 1902

Tarzan Luck

Born Chesterfield, Derbyshire, 1921

Micky Mouse

Married Dorothy Collett, Totternhoe,
Bedfordshire, 13 May 1641

Minnie Mouse

Born South Carolina *c.*1873 (Branchville,
South Carolina, 1880 US census)

Anne Muppet
Baptized St Nicholas, Brighton, Sussex, 12 October 1799

Cinderella Orange
Born Wakefield, Yorkshire, 1843

Peter Pan
Married Alice Legh, Chorley, Lancashire, 3 June 1700

Andy Pandy
Born c.1916 (Cow Lake, Arkansas, 1930 US census)
Andy Pandy was a puppet on a BBC TV series that started in 1950 and was revived in 2002.

Sue Perman
Born Wiltshire c.1791 (Downton,
Wiltshire, 1841 England census)

Harry Potter
Most of J. K. Rowling's characters have completely original names, but a few have real counterparts . . .

● ● ● ● ● ● ● ● ● ● ●

Harry Potter
Born Ashleyhay, Wirksworth, Derbyshire, 15 October 1690;
died 17 October 1713

Margaret Muggle
Married William Prosser, St Mary Somerset,
London, 21 January 1627

Hermione Granger
Born Washington, USA, 7 April 1911; died Los Angeles,
California, USA, 24 April 1986

Phineas Black
Born 21 October 1908; died St Johnsbury,
Vermont, USA, 22 February 1987

Reginald Cattermole
Born Norwich, Norfolk, 1875

Peter Pettigrew
Born West Derby, Lancashire, 1939

J. K. Rowling
Born Surrey 1958

*This is Julie K. Rowling, not to be confused with
Harry Potter author Joanne K. Rowling.*

Peter Rabbit
Baptized Hellingley, Sussex, 18 February 1648

Crusoe Robinson
Born Wortley, Yorkshire, 1888

Anastasia Shrek
Married Conrad Keifer, Erie, Ohio, USA, 23 August 1853

Dalek Smith
(Male) Born Georgia c.1889 (Decatur,
Georgia, 1910 US census)

Frank N. Stein
Born Indiana c.1857 (New Albany, Indiana, 1880 US census)

Flint Stone
(Male) Baptized Marsham, Norfolk, 12 September 1790

Batman Bin Suparman
Born Singapore 13 May 1990

Thomas Tank
Married Helston, Cornwall, 22 January 1792
(Cornwall Record Office)

Tom Thumb
Born Kentucky c.1859 (Bracken, Kentucky, 1860 US census)

Samuel Whiskers
Son of James and Mary Whiskers, baptized Inch,
Down, Ireland, 21 January 1794

Papa Bear Whitmore
Born 16 October 1927; died Wheat Ridge,
Colorado, USA, 22 October 2003

Doctor Who
Married Sonia Lowe, Lewisham, London, 1994

Ernest Womble Womble

Born Chesterfield, Derbyshire, 1908

Quasimodo W. T. Yeung

Born Leicester 1996
Quasimodo is the name of the title character in
The Hunchback of Notre Dame, *the 1831 novel by*
French author Victor Hugo.

The Seven Dwarfs

In the story of **Snow White and the Seven Dwarfs,**
none of the dwarfs had names until they were
invented for the 1937 Walt Disney film.

● ● ● ● ● ● ● ● ● ● ● ● ● ●

Snow White

Born 20 October 1914; died Union,
Georgia, USA, 18 October 1980

William Bashful

Baptized Bolstestone, Yorkshire, 11 January 1789

Dopey Dillard

Born Georgia *c.*1877 (Rockdale, Georgia, 1880 US census)

Lodewick Doc

Married Ann Nallor, Boston, Lincolnshire, 17 November 1663

Oliver Grumpy

Born California *c.*1905 (San Antonio,
California, 1910 US census)

Sleepy Jim

Born California *c.*1845 (Martins Ferry,
California, 1880 US census)

Happy Joy
Born 17 April 1887; died Philadelphia,
Pennsylvania, USA, April 1982

Bashful Mitchell
Born Arkansas c.1879 (L'Anguille, Arkansas, 1880 US census)

Fergus Sneezy
Born 23 February 1901; died San Carlos,
Arizona, USA, February 1981

The Simpsons

The Simpsons has been screened since 1987, making it the longest-running cartoon series ever. Some of the characters' names exist as those of real people.

● ● ● ● ● ● ● ● ● ● ● ● ● ●

Homer J. Simpson
Born 3 November 1907; died Landis,
North Carolina, USA, 16 December 1987

Marge Simpson
Born 18 August 1920; died Scranton,
Pennsylvania, USA, June 1987

Bart Simpson
Born c.1927 (Loudon, Tennessee, 1930 US census)

Lisa Simpson
Born 19 October 1956; died Bend, Oregon, USA, 31 July 2004

Maggie Simpson
Born 21 December 1887; died Cobb,
Georgia, USA, 26 March 1988

Patty Bouvier

Born 13 March 1897; died Lewiston,
Maine, USA, 18 January 1984

Kent Brockman

Born 23 December 1917; died West Virginia,
USA, 30 June 1997

Montgomery Burns

Born Kalamazoo, Michigan, USA, 22 October 1874

Carl Carlson

Baptized Viipuri, Finland, 14 June 1736

Maude Flanders

Born Iowa 1879 (Ellsworth, Kansas, 1900 US census)

Ned Flanders

Born New Hampshire 1859 (Manchester,
New Hampshire, 1900 US census)

Rod Flanders

Born Saint Louis, Minnesota, USA, 25 December 1946

Todd Flanders

Born Hennepin, Minnesota, USA, 9 October 1961

John Frink

Born Marlborough, Devon, 20 August 1639; died Stonington,
Connecticut, America, 8 December 1717

Barney Gumble

Born Kansas c.1878 (Salem, 1885 Kansas, USA, census)

Julius Hibbert

Born Wisconsin c.1879 (Dubuque, 1885 Iowa, USA, census)

Osper E. Krusty
Resident of Des Moines, Iowa (1905 Iowa, USA, census)

Lenny Leonard
Born Indiana c.1867 (Warren, Indiana, 1870 US census)

Helen Lovejoy
Born 27 June 1892; died Barnesville,
Ohio, USA, 21 June 1983

Timothy Lovejoy
Born 20 April 1953; died New Carlisle,
Ohio, USA, 7 December 2007

Troy McClure
Born 28 March 1891; died Marion,
Ohio, USA, 7 January 1970

Nelson Muntz
Born 2 May 1912; died Montgomery,
Ohio, USA, 29 March 1998

Joe Quimby
Baptized Clifton Campville, Staffordshire, 25 October 1853

Abraham Simpson
Baptized St Botolph's, London, 24 August 1625

Seymour Skinner
Born Onondaga, New York,
USA, 15 October 1831; died 9 June 1898

Even More Weird and Wonderful Names

22

Furious Andrews

(Female) Born Great Horwood, Buckinghamshire, *c.*1821
(Steeple Claydon, Buckinghamshire, 1881 England census)

Herbert Abcdef Atkinson

Born Tynemouth, Northumberland, 1904
'Abcdef' was his middle name, not his initials.

Crystal Ball

Born Nebraska *c.*1908 (Gage, Nebraska, 1920 US census)
*Her sister was called Merlin Ball – perhaps they
were a family of magicians.*

Earless Barber

Born 3 May 1897; died Lafayette, Tennessee, USA, May 1981

Lord Baron

Born Haslingden, Lancashire, 1842
'Lord' was his first name.

True Batts

Born 10 February 1903; died Kansas City,
Missouri, USA, April 1985

Hopalong Benford
Born Fayette, Texas, USA, 3 May 1943

Funny Sunny Blackshire
(Male) Born Louisiana, USA, 23 March 1883;
died Carthage, Texas, 29 February 1956

True Blue
Born 17 September 1888; died Lebo,
Kansas, USA, February 1972

Plummer Bodily
Born 8 November 1894; died Tennessee, USA, August 1964

Reader Book
Born Alabama 1899 (Fox Creek, Alabama, 1900 US census)

Oofty Goofty Bowman
Married Fannie Edwards, St Joseph, Indiana, USA, 9 May 1913

Wallop Brabazon
Married Jane Du Pre, St Marylebone, London, 19 March 1796

Merry Ann Bright
Born Tom Green county, Texas, USA, 21 March 1947

Gentle Bunch
Born 13 April 1907; died New Orleans,
Louisiana, USA, May 1968

Trixie Calamity
Born 28 December 1914; died Tonalea,
Arizona, USA, 24 July 1997

I. D. Card
(Female) Born Portsmouth, Hampshire, 1908

Justin Case
Born New York c.1832 (Bowne, Missouri, 1870 US census)

May Cheat
Born Maine c.1872 (Rockland, Maine, 1880 US census)

Tensil L. Cheesebrew
Born 2 October 1930; died Elberta,
Alabama, USA, 2 July 1998

Pleasant Child
Buried St Dunstan's, Canterbury, Kent, 21 December 1715

Melody Clinkenbeard
Born Bexar, Texas, USA, 18 January 1944

Ty Coon
Born c.1967; died Tacoma, Washington, USA, 21 May 1985

Magic Enchantress Creamer
Born 23 February 1974; died
California, USA, 3 December 2007

Lovie Crumblie
Born 18 February 1908; died Birmingham,
Alabama, USA, 27 June 1991

Dandridge Crumpecker
Married Constance Oglesby, Bedford,
Virginia, USA, 11 December 1850

Jemina [sic] Crysick
Resident of Warren, North Carolina (1790 US census)

Danger Dangervil
Born 29 June 1943; died Homestead,
Florida, USA, 23 November 2005

Zip A. Dee Doo Daub
Son of Vernon Daub and Betty Sue Adams,
born El Paso, Texas, USA, 18 October 1983

O. Dear
Born Stotfold, Bedfordshire, c.1886
(Stotfold, 1891 England census)

Darwin Dibble
Born Pennsylvania c.1851
(Bay City, Michigan, 1930 US census)

Sigourney May Gay Dibble
Born Glamorgan 2001

Lula Dingledine
Born Widdrington, Northumberland, 24 February 1872

Zip Dominion
Married Maureen Brown, Manchester, Lancashire, 1991

Wake Doom
Born Kentucky 1893 (Kuttawa Town,
Kentucky, 1900 US census)

Win Dow
Born Maldon, Essex, 1886

James Lord Drivel
Born Gildersome, Yorkshire, c.1848
(Leeds, Yorkshire, 1871 England census)

Dinah Dump
Born Whitechapel, London, 1897

Stan Dupp
Born c.1922; passenger on *Hubert Howe Bancroft*, Los Angeles, California–New York, USA, arrived 13 June 1945

Duke Earl
Born Alabama c.1905 (Riderwood, Alabama, 1930 US census)

Penelope Empty
Baptized St Mary's, Watford, Hertfordshire, 18 January 1723

Bobby Good Evans
Born Brighton, Sussex, 1985

Alice May Fall
Born Shoreditch, London, 1894

Dort Fauntleroy
Born Chicago, Illinois, 30 April 1925
(Geneva, Illinois, 1930 US census)

Ffaithfull Ffillips
Married Lanreath, Cornwall, 29 November 1660

Hiram Finnyfrock
Born Pennsylvania c.1856 (Eldred, Pennsylvania, 1880 US census)

Safety First
Born Pennsylvania, USA, 23 March 1894; died Seal Beach, Orange, California, USA, 20 April 1985
His sister June First was born in Pennsylvania in c.1905.

Olga Flabbi
Born 20 December 1918; died Johnston City, Illinois, USA, March 1972

Waldemar Floggie

Born 30 December 1904; died Jefferson,
Kentucky, USA, 5 January 1975

Adelaide Fluff

Born St Pancras, London, c.1867
(St Pancras, 1881 England census)

Effie Fogg

Married Leek, Staffordshire, 1895

G. Force

Born 12 December 1945; died Ohio, USA, 15 May 1990

Ellen Step Forward

Born East Stonehouse, Devon, 1846;
died Penzance, Cornwall, 1848

Earthmother Freeborn

Married Michael Eugene Robertson, Carson City, Nevada,
USA, 26 September 1995

Charming Frothingham

(Male) Born New York, USA, c.1882; passenger on
Queen Mary, Cherbourg, France–New York,
USA, arrived 25 April 1938

Capers Charles Funnye

Born 15 June 1929; died Cook County,
Illinois, USA, 5 September 1971

Sweetie Winifred Futter

Born Blofield, Norfolk, 1898

Ellie Gant

(Male) Born Tennessee *c.*1964 (Fayette, Tennessee, 1870 US census)

Pearly Gates

Married Kevin M. Cadle, Westminster, London, 1996

Big George

Died Guisborough, Yorkshire, 1871

John Farmer Giles

Born *c.*1881; died Witney, Oxfordshire, 1904

Princess Gladys Glastonbury

Born Keynsham, Somerset, 1902
'Princess' was her first name.

President Goggins

Born 3 March 1900; died Anniston, Alabama, USA, February 1981
'President' was his first name.

Been Googoo

(Male) Born 26 November 1874 (Whycocomagh, Nova Scotia, 1901 Canada census)

George Gorgeous

Born 24 March 1915; died Los Angeles, California, USA, 26 December 1963

Pea Green

Born Halifax, Yorkshire, 1856

Alice Haircut

Married Moses Cowcill, Deane, Lancashire, 27 February 1856

Ocellous Hardwick
Born 17 July 1893; died Adair,
Kentucky, USA, 21 October 1984

Oddity Harris
Born Droitwich, Worcestershire, c.1882 (Kings Norton,
Worcestershire, 1901 England census)

Hap Hazard
Born Illinois, USA, 22 August 1924; died Los Angeles,
California, 1 August 1979

Quasigreek N. Hebran
(Male) Born Manchester, Lancashire, c.1851
(Manchester, 1881 England census)

Milo B. High
Born 19 August 1926; died Memphis,
Tennessee, USA, 24 May 2007
He was the singer Elvis Presley's pilot.

Lightie Honker
Born 20 November 1890; died Dillon,
South Carolina, USA, February 1976

Annie How
Born Ecclesfield, Yorkshire, 1843

Mossie Husbands
Born 9 April 1911; died Gadsden, Florida, USA, 30 June 1971

Truly Irish
Born 28 February 1898; died St Louis,
Missouri, USA, December 1984

Question James
Born Williton, Somerset, 1880

Joy Jolly
Born 21 February 1938; died Biggleswade, Bedfordshire, 1991

Fay King
Born Colorado c.1915 (Baldy, Colorado, 1920 US census)

Shay King
Born 19 October 1947; died Charleston,
South Carolina, USA, May 1981

Delightful Knapp
Died Waupaca, Wisconsin, USA, 25 March 1901

Norbeth Koonce
Born 14 August 1908; died Nashville, Washington,
Illinois, USA, January 1974

Memory Lane
Born Alabama c.1875 (Limestone, Alabama, 1880 US census)

Magnolia Laughinghouse
Born North Carolina c.1879
(Chicoa, North Carolina, 1880 US census)

Aymyn Electric R. Lawrence
Born Pontypridd, Glamorgan, 1908

Zsi Zsi A. Le Scrooge
Born Hammersmith, London, 1990

Dee Light
Born 1964; died Hackney, London, 2004

Enormous Little
Born c.1950; died Shelby, North Carolina,
USA, 24 November 2007

Precious Little
Born 14 June 1944; died Los Angeles,
California, USA, 6 January 1982

Young Love
(Male) Born Donegal, Ireland, 29 March 1788;
died Pike, Ohio, USA, 20 May 1845

Thanks Luck
(Male) Born London *c.*1890
(South Weald, Essex, 1891 England census)

Ah Po Ah Ma
Born China *c.*1859 (Waimea, Hawaii, 1920 US census)

Frou-Frou Mallett
Born *c.*1904; died St Pancras, London, 1907

Hazzie McKnuckles
Born 18 December 1900; died Hamilton,
Mississippi, USA, August 1973

Mercedes D. McSwine
Born 23 January 1892; died Pine Bluff,
Arkansas, USA, February 1966

E. Pluribus Unum Medsker
(Female) Married Lone Rush (born Owen, Gosport, Indiana;
died 1963), Morgan, Indiana, USA, 14 September 1911
'E pluribus unum', Latin for 'Out of many, one',
is the motto of the United States.

Arthur Mind
Born Poplar, London, 1907

Major Minor
Born Arkansas *c.*1882 (Hot Springs, Arkansas, 1910 US census)

Arthur Minute
Born Hastings, Sussex, 1882

Owen Money
Born Headington, Oxfordshire, 1884

Les Moore
Born 1935; died Enfield, Middlesex, 2000

Miles More
Born Randwick, Gloucestershire, c.1824
(Standish, Gloucestershire, 1851 England census)

Cantwell F. Muckenfuss
Born 16 July 1910 (Summerville,
South Carolina, 1930 US census)

Henrietta Mug
Born Whitechapel, London, 1874

Gypsy Magical B. Nash
Born Kent 2005

Ruell Considerate Negus
Died Montpelier, Ohio, USA, 18 February 1909

Rachell Nude
Married Stephen Smith, Caister-on-Sea,
Norfolk, 20 November 1572

Submit Nutting
Married John Farrar, Pepperell, Massachusetts,
USA, 17 August 1815

Owen Slides Off
Married Elsie Clown, Ziebech,
South Dakota, USA, 4 December 1938

Captain Outrageous
Born 13 April 1940; died Key West,
Florida, USA, 10 February 2007

Red Paint
(Male) Born Wyoming c.1897
(Fremont, Wyoming, 1900 US census)

Easy Pease
Died Billericay, Essex, 1889

Emperor Pleasant
Born 28 May 1903; died New Orleans,
Louisiana, USA, September 1969

Noble Pluntz
Born 14 August 1915; died Shreveport,
Louisiana, USA, 10 June 1998

May Pole
Born Leicester 1904

Evangeline Polite
Born 25 October 1927; died Tampa,
Florida, USA, 16 March 1977

Roosevelt Polite
Born 17 October 1914; died Eutawville,
South Carolina, USA, June 1984
He was one of three Roosevelt Polites born in the
years 1907–14, named after Theodore Roosevelt,
US President 1901–09.

Nicknack Poole
Born Sheffield, Yorkshire, 1893

Henrietta Postman
Born Wisconsin c.1917 (Kenosha, Wisconsin, 1920 US census)

Max Power
Born Tredegar Park, Newport, Monmouthshire, *c.*1856
(Newport, 1881 Wales census)

Queen Prince
Died Chester, Cheshire, 1894
'Queen' was her first name.

Noble Puffer
Born 5 May 1901; died Palatine, Illinois, USA, April 1974

Wonky Purdom
(Female) Born Hoxton, London, *c.*1879 (Hemel Hempstead,
Hertfordshire, 1891 England census)

Harmonius [*sic*] Purity
Born 1 January 1900; died New York, USA, April 1979

Edwin Mowgwong Quack
Married St Pancras, London, 1861

Vanity Quackenbush
Born *c.*1906 (North Hempstead, New York, 1930 US census)

B. Quick
(Female) Born Ireland *c.*1822 (Tower Hamlets,
London, 1881 England census)

March Quick
Born Dakota *c.*1884 (Fayette, Pennsylvania, 1910 US census)

Love Reading
Baptized Rickmansworth, Hertfordshire, 20 November 1768

Cash Register
Born Florida 9 April 1946; died Burnsville,
Texas, USA, 19 February 1997

Wealthy Rich
Born Connecticut *c.*1776 (Strafford, Vermont, 1850 US census)

High Rockett
Married Bridport, Dorset, 1856

Roy Royalty
Born 21 July 1901; died Estil, Kentucky,
USA, 11 December 1971

Noah Sark
Born Indiana *c.*1882 (Bartlesville, Oklahoma, 1902 US census)

Dimple Semple
(Male) Born Southrepps, Norfolk, c.1860 (North Walsham, Norfolk, 1871 England census)

Major Senior Jr
Born South Carolina c.1924
(Sammy Swamp, South Carolina, 1930 US census)
And his father:

Major Senior Sr
Born South Carolina c.1890
(Sammy Swamp, South Carolina, 1930 US census)

Bob Sherunkle
Married Jane Walker, Colchester, Essex, 1992

Onabelle Shopbell
Born 1 February 1886; died Battle Creek, Michigan, USA, November 1968

Mary Winkle Shufflebotham
Born Macclesfield, Cheshire, 1843

Marriable F. Skipper
Born Oklahoma c.1916 (Miller, Oklahoma, 1920 US census)

Loveable Slater
Born Easington, Durham, 1899

Devil Smith
(Female) Born c.1816
(St Pancras, London, 1841 England census)

Warren Junior Snook
Born Nebraska 9 March 1924; died San Diego, California, USA, 17 October 1944

Hargood Snooke
Married Ann Foote, Stoke Damerel, Devon, 11 April 1780

Blondeen Sour
(Male) Born Pennsylvania c.1856 (Pittsburgh,
Pennsylvania, 1860 US census)

Spark Spinks
Born Thetford, Norfolk, 1840

Sidwella Splat
Married William Small, Chagford, Devon, 21 June 1613

Best Splatt
Baptized Whitestone, Devon, 2 July 1668

Martin Spreadeagle

Married Elizabeth Pitcher, St Mary in the Marsh,
Norwich, Norfolk, 22 July 1672

Sividious Vaden Starke Sr

Born 30 January 1890; died Roanoke Rapids,
North Carolina, USA, 19 July 1961

Pebble Stone

Born 8 January 1907; died Jackson, Florida, USA, 2 June 1998

Nicholas Streaker

Baptized St Oswald's, Durham, 27 October 1747

Lew Swires

Born Pennsylvania 1868 (Dean,
Pennsylvania, 1900 US census)

Ada Tantrum

Born Ludlow, Shropshire, 1875

Iris Tew

Born 1922; died Chester and Ellesmere Port, Cheshire, 1985
*Some people think this name sounds like 'Irish stew', others
hear it as 'I arrest you' in the name of the law.*

Old Book Thomspilie

Born Congleton, Cheshire, c.1863 (Hulme,
Lancashire, 1871 England census)

Fran Tick

Married Shoreditch, London, 1877

Frou-Frou Tilley

Born Bristol, Gloucestershire, c.1874 (Clifton,
Gloucestershire, 1881 England census)

Andy Tover
Born Warwickshire c.1821 (Birmingham,
Warwickshire, 1841 England census)

Benoni Trampleasure
Born Kingsbridge, Devon, 14 February 1815

Lucy Mysterious Trigg
Born Kensington, London, 1852

Prokey Tuddy
Born Austria c.1878 (Chicago, Illinois, 1920 US census)

Tsunami Blessingway Tyndall
(Female) Born Santa Barbara, California, USA, 25 July 1985

Elle Vator
Born Newhaven, Sussex, c.1858
(Brighton, Sussex, 1881 England census)

Never Wait

Born Manchester, Lancashire, c.1834 (Warrington, Lancashire, 1891 England census)

Isa Wake

(Female) Born North Shields, Durham, c.1863 (Gateshead, Durham, 1891 England census)

B. Ware

(Male) Born Pontypool, Monmouthshire, 1911

Winkle Weaver

(Female) Born North Carolina 1920 (Raleigh, North Carolina, 1920 US census)

Marvellous Webster

Married Todmorden, Yorkshire, 1861

Catherine Wheel

Born Auckland, Durham, 1867

Excepted Widdop

(Male) Born Ovenden, Yorkshire, c.1843 (Ovenden, 1881 England census)

Coyness Wiggins Jr

Married Jacqueline Orr, Williamson, Tennessee, USA, 7 March 1975

Brian Junior O. Willybiro

Born Southwark, London, 2001

Asad Experience Wilson

Born 1895; died Wasco, Oregon, USA, 3 November 1946

G. Wiss

(Male) Born Whitechapel, London, 1865

Minnie Woman
Born Caistor, Lincolnshire, 1891

Seldom Wright
(Male) Born Mississippi c.1880 (Memphis, Tennessee, 1910 US census)

B. Yond
(Male) Born Prescot, Lancashire, 1905

Barbara D. Zaster
Born Hochstadt, Odessa, Russia, 3 March 1834

Crazy Calendar

DAPPY DAYS

Any Day
Born Barningham, Suffolk, c.1857 (Crawshawbooth, Lancashire, 1871 England census)

Lucky Day
Born Blything, Suffolk, 1859

Nighten Day
(Male) Born Kentucky c.1804 (Cape Girardeau, Missouri, 1850 US census)

Selby Day
Born Ashton-under-Lyne, Lancashire, 1897

Time Of Day
(Male) Born Hoo, Kent, 1899

Tom Morrow
Born Stowe, Buckinghamshire, c.1854 (Camberwell, London, 1861 England census)

Tamara Knight
Born 21 August 1947; died Grayville, Illinois, USA, 2 July 2005

Monday Monday
(Male) Born Pennsylvania c.1857 (Philadelphia,
Pennsylvania, 1880 US census)

Tuesday Victory
(Male) Born Georgia c.1880 (Jamestown,
Georgia, 1880 US census)

Wednesday Nero
(Male) Born South Carolina c.1885 (Motts,
South Carolina, 1930 US census)

Thursday King
(Female) Born Poulstead, Suffolk (St Giles Cripplegate,
London, 1851 England census)

Friday Monday
(Male) Born Georgia c.1906 (Ware, Georgia, 1910 US census)

Saturday Merchant
Born Llandilofawr, Carmarthenshire, 1901

Sunday Ta Ta
(Male) Born Africa c.1876 (Garston,
Lancashire, 1881 England census)

MAD MONTHS
• • • • • • • • • • •

January Stringer
(Female) Born Norton, Suffolk, c.1842 (Wortley in Bramley,
Yorkshire, 1881 England census)

February Arney

Born Poole, Dorset, *c*.1886 (Poole, 1901 England census)
*February's mother was called Thursday Arney. She also had a
younger sister called Thursday.*

March May

(Female) Born Middlesex *c*.1817 (St George in the East,
London, 1841 England census)

April May

Born *c*.1920 (Miami, Oklahoma, 1930 US census)

May June

Born Greenwich, Kent, *c*.1808
(Greenwich, 1851 England census)

June July

Born Alabama *c*.1812
(Montgomery Hill, Alabama, 1880 US census)

July August

Born Georgia *c*.1842 (Savannah, Georgia, 1870 US census)

August June

(Male) Born Germany *c*.1846
(Queens, New York, 1880 US census)

September Smith

Married Elizabeth Ditchburn, South Shields, Durham, 1912

October Pudney

Born Woolwich, London, 1893

November Fish

Born 24 November 1903; died Wamego,
Kansas, USA, February 1995

December Storms

(Female) Born 22 December 1927; died Santa Cruz, California, USA, 22 December 1980

ZANY ZODIAC
• • • • • • • • • • •

Aries Busson
Married Robert Parker, Old Church,
St Pancras, London, 27 September 1807

Taurus Savage
Born Wisconsin 1875 (Walnut Grove,
Minnesota, 1900 US census)

Gemini Ragsdale
(Female) Born c.1916 (Cherokee, Texas, 1930 US census)

Cancer Grindsstaff
(Female) Born Tennessee c.1859
(Blount, Tennessee, 1880 US census)

Leo Lion
Born West Derby, Lancashire, 1892

Virgo Birks
(Male) Born 4 April 1826; baptized Old Church,
St Pancras, London, 3 May 1826

Libra Waterfall
(Female) Born Foleshill, Warwickshire, c.1803
(Foleshill, 1861 England census)

Scorpio Newman
(Male) Born Isleworth, Middlesex, c.1865
(Isleworth, 1881 England census)

Sagittarius Bobino
Married Emmanuella O. Osadebay, Harris,
Texas, USA, 30 January 1997

Capricorn Panetta
Born 16 January 1950; died Parkersburg,
West Virginia, USA, 28 July 2007

Aquarius Fynes
(Male) Baptized Frithville, Lincolnshire, 27 February 1825

Pisces Agostini
Born c.1875; passenger on *Yarra*, arrived Sydney,
New South Wales, Australia, 28 March 1906

ROUND THE YEAR
• • • • • • • • • • • • • • • •

New Year Beadle
(Female) Married James Theaker, Thorne, Lincolnshire, 1862

Happy New Year Kapahu
Born Hawaii c.1907 (Lihue, Hawaii, 1910 US census)

New Year Womble
(Male) Born North Carolina c.1865
(Parine, Florida, 1910 US census)

Valentine Card
(Male) Born 1913; died Chelmsford, Essex, 1993

Valentine Day
Born Leeds, Yorkshire, 1842

Coy Valentine
Born 19 January 1907; died Edenton,
North Carolina, USA, August 1983

Shrove Tuesday
(Male) Born Africa c.1859
(on Royal Navy ship *Euryalus*, 1881 England census)

Easter Bunny
(Female) Born Yorkshire c.1826
(Bradford, Yorkshire, 1841 England census)

Luscious Easter
Born 4 August 1915; died Cleveland, Ohio, USA, March 1979

Esther Egg
Married Glanford Brigg, Lincolnshire, 1863

Easter Loony
Baptized Maughold, Isle of Man, 11 November 1744

May Day
Died Axbridge, Somerset, 1842

May Holiday
Born Westminster, London, 1878

Summer Long
(Male) Born New Hampshire c.1848
(Conway, New Hampshire, 1850 US census)

John Halloween
Baptized St Nicholas', Liverpool, Lancashire, 13 June 1852

Halloween Hildebrand
Married James Loy Waltrip, Bloomfield,
Missouri, USA, 25 August 1933

Happy Holiday
(Female) Born Hardingham, Norfolk, c.1829
(Wymondham, Norfolk, 1851 England census)

CHRISTMAS
• • • • • • • • • •

William Christmas Angel
Born Flegg, Norfolk, 1890

Christmas Balls
Born Docking, Norfolk, 1886

Jingle Bell
Married Don Bradley, Hopkins, Texas, USA, 1 February 1975

Holly Berry
Born Barnsley, Yorkshire, 1880

Thomas William Christmas Bo
Born Gravesend, Kent, 1864

Holly Bush
Born Southampton, Hampshire, 1899

Eva Carol Christmas
Born 1919; died Corby, Northamptonshire, 2003

Eve Christmas
Died Stockport, Cheshire, 1859

Merry Christmas
Born Midhurst, Sussex, 1874

Santa Claus
Born 10 June 1930; died Reidsville, North Carolina, USA,
10 September 2008

Christmassy B. Cross
Born Woodbridge, Suffolk, 1926

Christmas Day
(Male) Baptized Lowestoft, Suffolk, 27 December 1762

Mistletoe Ellis
Born and died Aston, Warwickshire, 1906

Christmas Eve Gooch
Born Norwich, Christmas Eve 1853

Christmas Holiday
Married Ampthill, Bedfordshire, 1864

Ivy Holly
Born Eastbourne, Sussex, 1891

Silent Knight
Baptized Dorchester, Dorset, 24 December 1607

Fairy Light
(Male) Born Tennessee c.1896
(Dyer, Tennessee, 1910 US census)

Wayne Manger
Born Pennsylvania c.1877
(Reading, Pennsylvania, 1910 US census)

Chris Mass
Born Asenby, Yorkshire, c.1839
(Lamesley, Durham, 1861 England census)

Christmas Meringue
Born Italy c.1877 (Brazos, Texas, 1910 US census)

Christmas Merry
Born Williton, Somerset, 1885

Saint Nicholas
Baptized Aldbourne, Wiltshire, 3 February 1663

Runny Rudolf
Born Pennsylvania 1900 (Philadelphia,
Pennsylvania, 1900 US census)

Christmas Rush
Born Norfolk *c*.1801 (Norwich, Norfolk, 1841 England census)

Carol Service
Born 20 October 1932; died Willington,
Connecticut, USA, 14 April 1997

A. Carol Singer
Born Ipswich, Suffolk, 1993

Christmas White
Born Boston, Lincolnshire, 1858

Christmas Windy
Baptized St Augustine, Norwich, Norfolk, 27 December 1778

Mary Xmas
Baptized Petworth, Sussex, 10 December 1759

John Yuletide
Baptized St Luke's, Leek, Staffordshire, 1879

Anna Partridge (in a pear tree ... ?)
Married John Adams, Aldenham, Hertfordshire, 29 April 1562

ASTONISHING AFTERTHOUGHTS

*Especially in the nineteenth century, people
often had large families – the children's writer
Edward Lear, for example, was the 20th in his family.
Sometimes, parents gave their latest child a name that suggests
they had had enough – one, it was claimed, was even
called 'That's It Who'd Have Thought It Restell', but
his or her birth has not yet been proved.*

● ●

Not Wanted Carroll

Born Ohio 1850 (Brush Creek, Ohio, 1850 US census)
*Not Wanted was the newborn ninth child of
Enoch and Elizabeth Carroll.*

Last Child

(Male) Born Runham, Norfolk, c.1866
(Great Yarmouth, Norfolk, 1871 England census)
*He was not in fact the last child of Henry and Susanna Child,
but the fifth of six.*

Not Wanted James Colvill

Born (and died) Lambeth, London, 1861

No More Durrant

Born Risbridge, Suffolk, 1899

Worthy Extra

Married Malmesbury, Wiltshire, 1865

Errata Ford

(Female) Born Indiana c.1880

(Washington, Indiana, 1880 US census)

'Errata' are a list of mistakes, such as those in a book. Errata Ford was the youngest of the six children of farm labourer James and Mary Ford.

One Too Many Gouldstone

Born West Ham, Essex, 1870

Addition Lang

(Female) Born Ontario, Canada, 1 July 1896

Addition was the fifth child of farmer Garrett and Ellen Lang – who then had three more, including twins James and Theresa.

Finis London

(Male) Born Barking, Essex, c.1890

(Barking, 1891 England census)

Finis, which means 'the end', was he last of the seven children of Alfred and Mary London.

Appendix Lowder

Born Kentucky c.1868 (Old Town,
Greenup, Kentucky, 1880 US census)

An appendix is something that has been added, but Appendix was only the second of the five children of George and Josephine Lowder.

Addenda Morse

Born Kentucky c.1865 (Lewis, Kentucky, 1870 US census)

Addenda (which means additions) had a sister called Appends (added).

Final Edwin Preston

(Male) Born Market Bosworth, Leicestershire, 1892
Final was, they hoped, the last-born of the six children of Lot and Amy Preston.

Lewis Unexpected Smith

Born Medway, Kent, 1899

Too Many Whitehead

Born North Carolina 1880 (Swift Creek,
North Carolina, 1880 US census)
Too Many was the latest of Allen and Lucinda Whitehead's six children.

Enough Wright

(Male) Born Shropshire c.1835 (South Bradford,
Shropshire, 1841 England census)
*Charles and Margret [sic] Wright named their eighth son
'Enough' – but then had another, Moses, and a daughter, Mary.*

Supplement Zepp

Born Germany 1848 (St Louis, Missouri, 1900 US census)

AMAZING AMERICANS

In the United States of America, official public records often include strange names. We have no way of checking whether these were the names with which people were born, or if they have changed them to attract attention, nor do we know where or when they were born, so this selection is presented without the sort of information in the rest of the book.

● ●

Little David Bean
Santa Beans
Tina Beans
Ridgely Ridgely Biddle
Rusty Bolt
Windy Bottoms
Sparkle Bright
Moses Bullrush
Windy T. Bump
Orangejello Castleberry
Prince Charming
Dr Natwarlal Cholera
C. Q. Cumber
Barbie Doll
Ima Dork
Crescent Dragonwagon

Natalie Drest
Ann Droid
Nigel Earthworm III
Derail Easter
Rhoda Eligator
Goble Fogle
Rick Go Forth
Kermit The Frog
Juliet Seashell Moonbeam Gamba
Max Headroom
Becautious Hunter
Tanya Hyde
Tonsillitis S. Jackson
Northwinds Reindeer Liama
Ima Looney
Filthy McNasty
Sunshine Mink
Turmoil Morris
Rusty Nail
Jack B. Nimble
Fred Nitwit
Wong Numba
Gracious Outlaw
Freaky Parker
Stanley Shamp Poo
Merlin Prance
Optimus Prime

Bunny Rabbit
Lemonjello Snarfblat
Mona Lisa Spearmint
Chuck Stones
Justin Time
Hyacinthus Turnipseed
Alison Wonderland
Noah Zark

Acknowledgements

I would like to thank the writers, researchers and archivists who kindly shared their name discoveries with me, including: William Bell, John Benson, Helen Bickley, Claire Bolster, Nikki Bosworth, David Bowcock, Martin Cartwright, Richard Childs, James Collett-White, Paul Dickson, Dave Feakes, Liz Grant, John Harnden, Alison Healey, Renée Jackaman, A. Munro, Pauline Nash, Caroline Picco, Mike Rogers, Gill Shapland, Richard Smout, Roy Stockdill, Gerry Toop, Bonnie West and Eleanor Winyard.